Praise for *Insurgence*

"In this insightful and transformative book, Frank Viola reveals with crystal clarity just how far removed our truncated gospel is from the kingdom of God that Jesus embodied and that He calls and empowers His followers to embody. I am convinced that this wisdom-packed book will be used by God to completely transform the lives of many who dare to read it."

Greg Boyd, pastor and author

"Let me be clear—*Insurgence: Reclaiming the Gospel of the Kingdom* is not a book offering yet another parochial debate over some inconsequential point of theology. On the contrary, Viola's message strikes at the heart of the core message of Christianity."

Dr. Michael S. Heiser, biblical scholar and author

"I own thousands of books, but there's a very small handful of books that I keep on my desk to reread and refer to on a regular basis. Frank Viola's *Insurgence: Reclaiming the Gospel of the Kingdom* is one of those books. This isn't just a book—it's a revelation of how we as Christians should be living our lives in today's culture. Get the book. It will dramatically change how you look at the rest of your life."

Phil Cooke, filmmaker, media consultant, author

"*Insurgence* is a course corrective for the communication of the good news of Jesus. Thank you, Frank Viola, for masterfully presenting the gospel of Jesus as the here-and-now good news of the kingdom."

Bruxy Cavey, pastor and author

"*Insurgence* commands attention with its forthright, compelling vision of the kingd⟨   ⟩cets of the kingdom message."

Cr⟨   ⟩and author

Praise for *God's Favorite Place on Earth*

"Frank Viola's *God's Favorite Place on Earth* is a fast-moving, groundbreaking look at the Christian's struggle against legalism, discouragement, doubt, rejection, and spiritual complacency. A masterfully engaging book."

Mark Batterson, author and pastor

"A lot of people write books; Frank writes stories, and in this one we once again see why he's such a master. Honored to call him a friend, excited to call him an author I love to read."

Jon Acuff, author and blogger

"Frank Viola's pen and voice are consistently both penetrating and trustworthy."

Jack Hayford, renowned pastor and author

"Frank continues to challenge the church-at-large with a powerful mind, an impassioned voice, and a love for the Bride of Christ."

Ed Stetzer, author and speaker

"As masterly as a Cézanne canvas or a Stravinsky score, Frank Viola surpasses himself in his best book yet—a work of serene, soaring magnificence. Part novel, part biography, part theology, part Bible study, Frank's imaginative touch and command of prose haiku leaves the reader resolved more than ever to be a Bethany— God's favorite place on earth."

Leonard Sweet, author, seminary professor, speaker

"*God's Favorite Place on Earth* beautifully creates a powerful and moving portrait of the humanness of Jesus and His dearest relationships. Taking a story well told, Frank Viola engages the voice and view of Lazarus to bring a new perspective and moving relatability to Jesus' life on earth. Incredibly thoughtful and moving."

Jenni Catron, author and leadership consultant

"Few authors challenge me in my faith like Frank Viola. This book and the stories it contains will force you to face the myth of religion and instead adopt a life of deeper dedication to God, to find your own Bethany. It sure did for me."

Jeff Goins, author and blogger

Praise for *From Eternity to Here*

"Frank's *From Eternity to Here* is a masterpiece. . . . It reads like a movie on paper."

Dr. Myles Munroe, author and speaker

"When you're as old as I am, you don't hear new stuff. You can hardly say anything about religion that I haven't heard several times. But what's in *From Eternity to Here* is so new to me."

Steve Brown, author and talk-radio show host

"A great work of narrative theology."

Alan Hirsch, author and speaker

"Dissent is a gift to the church. It is the imagination of the prophets that continually calls us back to our identity as the peculiar people of God. May Viola's words challenge us to become the change that we want to see in the church."

Shane Claiborne, author and activist

"I just finished *From Eternity to Here*. I'm in process of reading it again. It has moved into my top ten books. Brilliant."

Derwin Gray, pastor and author

Praise for *Jesus Manifesto*

"There cannot be enough books written about the majesties and excellencies of Christ. I am grateful that Frank and Leonard Sweet put *Jesus Manifesto* in the lap of so many."

Matt Chandler, pastor and author

"Whether you are a seminary professor or someone seeking answers about Christ for the first time, *Jesus Manifesto* promises to illuminate the truth about the greatest personality to ever walk the earth."

Ed Young, pastor and author

"If we follow the Spirit, Christ can become as real to us as the world was when we were sinners. *Jesus Manifesto* is a compass pointing toward this holy pursuit."

Francis Frangipane, pastor and author

"*Jesus Manifesto* is a passionate invitation to fall head over heels in love with the Son of God. Prepare to be shaken. Prepare to be awakened. And prepare to answer the call to follow Jesus with wholehearted abandon. After reading this book, you'll never be the same."

Margaret Feinberg, author and speaker

"*Jesus Manifesto* is the most powerful work on Christ I have read in recent years. The Christ of the Empty Tomb is back among us. Sweet and Viola have beckoned us to return to Olivet and renew our souls. I was hushed by its welcome authority. I found a lump in my throat as I read through page after page of biblical witness to the one and only, incomparable Christ in whom alone is our Salvation. You must read this book. All of us must, and then we must believe in this book, rise, and advance on our culture with the truth we have lately backed away from in our faulty attempt to play fair at the cost of our God-given mission."

Calvin Miller, author and professor

"Brilliant, refreshing, soaring—and that's just the first chapter! This book is destined to be a classic devotional volume that will inspire generations of Jesus-followers. The line from the song goes, 'You can have all this world, but give me Jesus.' This book does just that."

Reggie McNeal, author and missional specialist

Praise for *The Day I Met Jesus*

"What a treasure this diary-style book—*The Day I Met Jesus*—is!"

Lysa TerKeurst, author and speaker

"Jesus, from the very beginning, has been 'good news for women.' One reads of His encounters with the women described in *The Day I Met Jesus* with a sense of wonder that these interactions took place two thousand years ago. He is good news for women still."

John Ortberg, pastor and author

"I thought I knew the women in these stories well, but in this beautiful book—*The Day I Met Jesus*—I met each one in a fresh, personal, and profound way."

Sheila Walsh, author and speaker

"We all long to lift the veil of history and catch a glimpse of the real story—the one that makes our hearts pound, our faith grow, and our lives change. You will never look at Scripture or God's work in your own heart the same way again after you close the final page."

Holley Gerth, author

ReGRACE

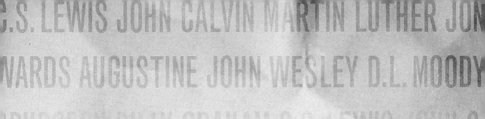

ReGRACE

What the SHOCKING BELIEFS
of the Great Christians
Can Teach Us Today

FRANK VIOLA

BakerBooks

a division of Baker Publishing Group
Grand Rapids, Michigan

Published by Baker Books
a division of Baker Publishing Group
PO Box 6287, Grand Rapids, MI 49516-6287
www.bakerbooks.com

Printed in the United States of America

Library of Congress Cataloging-in-Publication Data
Names: Viola, Frank, author.
Title: ReGrace : what the shocking beliefs of the great Christians can teach us today / Frank Viola.
Description: Grand Rapids : Baker Publishing Group, 2019. | Includes bibliographical references.
Identifiers: LCCN 2018043227 | ISBN 9780801077159 (pbk.)
Subjects: LCSH: Theology—History. | Church history.
Classification: LCC BR118 .V56 2019 | DDC 230—dc23
LC record available at https://lccn.loc.gov/2018043227

In keeping with biblical principles of creation stewardship, Baker Publishing Group advocates the responsible use of our natural resources. As a member of the Green Press Initiative, our company uses recycled paper when possible. The text paper of this book is composed in part of post-consumer waste.

19 20 21 22 23 24 25   7 6 5 4 3 2 1

Contents

1

Why This Book?

The devil is a better theologian than any of us and is
a devil still.

~ A. W. Tozer

In November 2014, Rick Warren asked me to write a series
of blog posts on the shocking beliefs of the great Christians
who shaped the church (especially the evangelical wing).*

Warren's hope was that the series would "soften" the
uncivil climate in the Christian community over doctrinal
differences.

If, for example, a Christian discovered that his or her
theological "hero" had some peculiar, inaccurate, or even
shocking belief(s), this would give him or her pause before

*While I claim the term *evangelical* myself, because it best fits my theological
views, I don't stay within my corner of evangelicalism when it comes to reading
the writings of others. I also believe that modern evangelicalism has a number of
blind spots, something I've addressed on my blog—frankviola.org.

unloading both barrels on a fellow believer over an alleged doctrinal trespass.

After watching the nonstop carnage on social media over theological disagreements during the last decade, I fully resonated with Warren's goal. And so I began writing the "shocking beliefs" series on my blog.

Within a year, the series went viral, receiving hundreds of thousands of pageviews from all over the world.

In 2017, I had a conversation with the Baker publishing team about revising and expanding the series into a book. They agreed, and that's how this project began.

The Purpose of This Book

The book I wrote before the one you're reading right now is called *Insurgence: Reclaiming the Gospel of the Kingdom*— which is a fresh presentation of the earth-shaking gospel of the kingdom of God.*

One of the lessons those of us who have joined the Insurgence have learned is to always walk in the love of Christ, even toward people with whom we disagree.

> And the Lord's servant must not be quarrelsome but must be kind to everyone, able to teach, not resentful. (2 Timothy 2:24)

ReGrace has but one objective: to foster grace, civility, and tolerance among Christians when they disagree with one another over theological matters.

The subtitle "shocking" is subjective. Some Christians will find a number of the beliefs articulated in this book to

---

*Frank Viola, *Insurgence: Reclaiming the Gospel of the Kingdom* (Grand Rapids: Baker, 2017). Many have called *Insurgence* my "signature work."

be first-class shockers. Others will find them surprising. A small number may shrug their shoulders and muse to themselves, "So what?"

Yet the point made in each chapter is undeniable. No influential Christian of the past could claim flawless perception. Each of them had blind spots. Some of their views were peculiar at best. Others were aberrant or ran contrary to Scripture, at least to the minds of many evangelical Christians.

But despite their less-than-perfect beliefs, God still used them.

This fact alone should cause us to relax whenever we run into a teacher, preacher, author, or fellow Christian on a blog or social media feed who holds views with which we disagree.

Especially when we come to grips with the immovable fact that none of us is immune to being wrong.

That includes you and me.

Getting Clear

Before we move on, I want to be crystal clear about five things:

1) There's no reason to get offended with any of the chapters in this book. Unless of course, you're easily offended. (If that's the case, I have no guaranteed antidote for you, but I did address you directly in a previous book with a cure.)†

2) Most Christians have heroes. I know I do. But some people are overly protective of theirs. I was keenly aware

---

†Frank Viola, *God's Favorite Place on Earth* (Colorado Springs: David C. Cook, 2013).

of this when I wrote the blog post on the "Shocking Beliefs of John Calvin." After I published it, I sent this email to Rick Warren:

> **Subject:** Shocking Beliefs of John Calvin (this one may get me hung!)
>
> Hi Rick. The post is below. If I disappear, it's your fault!
>
> You can reach me at Salman Rushdie's place. ;-)

Rick's response made me laugh out loud. He promised to officiate my funeral if my body was ever found!

Keep in mind that I'm not a "Calvin-hater." I never touched his theological system. I simply pointed out some beliefs he held that are shocking to many evangelical Christians, just as I did with the rest of the people I treat in this volume.

Nevertheless, in response to that original blog post, I was on the receiving end of hate mail. Even from Quakers! The smoldering anger laden in those emails would make Keyser Söze blush. (If you don't know who Mr. Söze is, you can insert Howard Stern into that sentence.)

What do I mean? Here are two of the tamer ones (*cough*):

> Viola's journey to the dark side is now complete. Writing this blog post is the equivalent of witchcraft. I wonder if he's stopped torturing small animals too. Doubt it. Take me off his blog list immediately.

> Your "shocking beliefs" series reminds me of Charles Manson. You're a [expletive] and probably a closet serial killer too!

3) Some of the so-called shocking beliefs that I cover in this book are beliefs that I myself agree with. Others I find abhorrent. Consequently, just because a shocking belief is listed doesn't reveal how I personally feel about it. It simply means that many evangelical Christians will find the belief to be shocking (at worst) or peculiar (at best).

Therefore, to those of you who are inclined to finish this book and proudly throw your chest out saying, "Good grief, I wasn't shocked by any of those beliefs!" remember three things: You missed the point of the book; each person I feature had people who believed they were heretics during their day; and every one of them still have people raking them over the coals because of their viewpoints.

4) While I disagree with a number of beliefs that each person I feature held, I have respect for each of them. In fact, I cannot tie the laces of their shoes. Each individual was remarkable in his own right. I realize this means that people who don't like Calvin, Lewis, Wesley, Augustine, and so forth will be turned off by that statement. *And some may misuse this book as a frontal attack on each person it covers, completely missing the boat on those chapters and the intent of this volume.* If you ever find someone doing that, feel free to quote this paragraph to them to jar their memory.

5) To keep this book relatively short, I didn't cover *every* shocking belief these figures from church history held. I simply covered the beliefs I felt were sufficient to make my point. The source materials will give you further information about each individual and their views. So I'm

sure you can uncover more of their shocking beliefs, if you desire to investigate. But again, how many peculiar views they held isn't the point. The point is that some of their beliefs were imperfect, and hence, we should show more tolerance toward each other whenever we disagree.

On "Great" Christians

For the both of you who are apoplectic right now because I used the word "great" to describe fallen humans, let me point out that I'm merely following Jesus here (emphasis mine):

> The *greatest* among you will be your servant. (Matthew 23:11)

> Truly I tell you, among those born of women there has not risen anyone *greater* than John the Baptist; yet whoever is least in the kingdom of heaven is *greater* than he. (Matthew 11:11)

> Whoever practices and teaches these commands will be called *great* in the kingdom of heaven. (Matthew 5:19)

So settle down, okay?

Note that I'm only covering eight "great Christians" in this book. In my study of church history, these are the people I believe shaped the evangelical Christian world the most. I don't have a "shocking belief" entry for Billy Graham since I don't think he fits into that category. However, I did feature seven surprising (perhaps even shocking) quotes by him.

You will find that no women are featured. That's because in my research, the women who significantly shaped church history (such as Fanny Crosby and Amy Carmichael) didn't appear to hold to any shocking beliefs.* I suppose that's a compliment to them.

Finally, I've deliberately omitted the shocking actions of the great Christians, focusing instead on their beliefs (actions and beliefs aren't the same).

It bears repeating: the purpose of this book is not to lower these individuals in your eyes. It's actually the opposite. It's to show you that despite their strange (and sometimes flawed) thinking on some issues, God still used them. Mightily, even.

The lesson, of course, is that God uses His people in spite of their strange or erroneous perspectives. And since that's the case, let's have more grace whenever we disagree with one another.

It's time for us to regrace.†

---

*Carmichael dressed like the Native American women she ministered to and allegedly kidnapped children who were being sold as sex slaves (in an effort to rescue them). She also didn't accept donations. But none of these beliefs would be shocking or surprising to a twenty-first-century Christian audience.

†By *regrace*, I simply mean *re*thinking and *re*discovering God's *grace* in relation to those with whom we disagree. In other words, to begin to be *gracious* toward all our fellow sisters and brothers in Christ, especially when we don't see eye to eye.

2

'Tis Humor

All along, let us remember we are not asked to understand, but simply to obey.

~ Amy Carmichael

When I began my "shocking beliefs" blog series that eventually became this book, I anticipated that some readers would misuse a post to attack the Christians I was covering.

Others wanted to roast me over a slow spit after they realized their spiritual hero didn't possess immaculate perception.

For these reasons, I added this caution just before the comment section that followed each blog post. This one appeared under the C. S. Lewis post:

WARNING: Now that you have been made aware of some of the surprising beliefs of C. S. Lewis, you may be tempted to overreact. So before you write your comment, heed this warning: If anyone wields accusations like "C. S. Lewis is the mouthpiece of Satan" or "Lewis is a cross between the Antichrist, the Zodiak killer, and the Unabomber" and other such sentiments, our beloved Blog Manager won't approve the comment.

So those of you who found this post on the web somewhere and are starting to march toward the comments box with pitchforks, blowtorches, and blunt objects in order to delegitimize, castigate, or marginalize Lewis beyond repair, your remark will vanish into the electricity after the Blog Manager hits the Delete key.

In addition, this isn't the place for a theological smackdown, a doctrinal beatdown, a "look how much I know about C. S. Lewis" ego session, or a Calvinism vs. Arminianism feeding frenzy. We simply ask that you post your favorite C. S. Lewis quote in the comments. Thank you very much.

3

We Know in Part

It is only with the heart that one can see rightly; what
is essential is invisible to the eye.

~ Antoine de Saint-Exupéry

As I argued in *Revise Us Again*,[1] every follower of Jesus is a
rough draft. Over time, the great Editor—the Holy Spirit—
shapes our lives and views. But until we see the Lord, and
we "know even as we are known," we are all in process.*

This is also true for the great Christians who have gone
before us.

Therefore, one of the mistakes we should guard against
is the temptation to dismiss a person's entire contribution
because they may hold (or have held) to ideas we find difficult to stomach.

---

*This is a reference to Paul's words in 1 Corinthians 13:12: "For now we see
through a glass, darkly; but then face to face: now I know in part; but then shall
I know even as also I am known" (KJV).

Speaking personally, if I demanded that a person's theological views be identical to mine, then if I met myself thirty years ago, I would have had to disfellowship myself!

The truth is, my views on some topics have changed over the years.

And so have yours.

We are all in process. None of us gets everything right all the time. This stands true for every Christian who has ever breathed oxygen.

So my purpose in highlighting some of the shocking beliefs of the people upon whose shoulders we stand is *not* to burn them in effigy. Nor is it to dismiss their positive contributions to church history.

Rather, it's to demonstrate that even though they may have held views that would raise the eyebrows (or the ire) of many Christians today, that doesn't overturn nor negate the valuable ideas they contributed to the body of Christ.

Unfortunately, many evangelicals are quick to discount—and even damn—their fellow brothers and sisters over alleged doctrinal trespasses, even if those same brothers and sisters hold to the historical orthodox creeds (Apostles' Creed, Nicene Creed, etc.). But such discounting serves no one on the kingdom side of the aisle, and it can be avoided.

When diversity within orthodoxy is encountered, grace should be extended. Just as we would want grace extended to us, seeing that none of us sees perfectly (Matthew 7:12). Therefore, we should never judge the whole bag by one or two grains of wheat.*

---

*Later in the book, I will address what constitutes orthodox Christian belief and how we should treat those who teach doctrines that contradict it. In other words, I'll discuss "heresy" and those who promote false doctrines.

The words of Paul of Tarsus contain thunder and lightning on this score:

> Now our knowledge is partial and incomplete. (1 Corinthians 13:9 NLT)

Or in the words of the NKJV, we "know in part."

4

Honoring Those with Whom You Disagree

I have decided to stick with love. Hate is too great a
burden to bear.

~ Martin Luther King Jr.

We've all seen it. The belligerent throwdowns where Christians take the gloves off with fellow believers over doctrinal, theological, and political differences.

Many of them can't walk away from a fight or lose. Instead, they either pour coals on an already roaring fire or they bring in the gasoline trucks.

For this reason, it's time for us to recover the lost art of agreeing to disagree.

The devil gloats when God's children are at one another's throats over their petty disagreements. But forfeiting a relationship over a disagreement effectively dismantles the words of Jesus:

> By this everyone will know that you are my disciples, if you love one another. (John 13:35)

> That they may be brought to complete unity. Then the world will know that you sent me. (John 17:23)

John Wesley was the first to put the phrase "agree to disagree" in print in the eighteenth century. George Whitefield was his sparring partner, and Wesley attributes the phrase to him. Here's the quote:

> If you agree with me, well: if not, we can, as Mr. Whitefield used to say, agree to disagree.[1]

In light of the doctrinal disagreements between Wesley (an Arminian) and Whitefield (a Calvinist), someone once asked Whitefield if he thought he'd see John Wesley in heaven. Here is Whitefield's reply:

> I fear not, for he will be so near the eternal throne and we at such a distance, we shall hardly get sight of him.[2]

This statement reveals the spiritual stature of George Whitefield.

To recognize the place of another servant of God in the kingdom despite doctrinal disagreements is an evidence of a person who walks with God.

To speak well of another servant of God, honoring them in public even, is a mark of spiritual greatness and Christlike humility. This is especially true when we have significant disagreements with their theology (or their politics).*

*I, of course, am not speaking about what the Scriptures call "false teaching" or "heresy." I treat those kinds of erroneous beliefs in another part of the book. But God even uses heresies and false teachings for good, despite the harm they

To have the insight to see when God's hand is on a person and using them, despite the doctrinal differences we may have with them, is a sign of someone who knows the Lord well. Whitefield's remark about Wesley is rare to see in our day where bickering, casting aspersions, and dismissing (in particular) are the order of the day when it comes to theological disagreements among Christian leaders.

Let's take our cue from Wesley and Whitefield when encountering a disagreement with a fellow believer. Learn the art of agreeing to disagree. When it comes to countless doctrinal, theological, and political disagreements, most of those hills aren't worth dying on.

(Indeed, there are times when we should dig in our heels on a point of orthodoxy, but not to the point of violence—either physical or verbal. We'll explore this matter later in the book.)

May Whitefield's tribe increase!

---

bring. Samuel Bolton's *The Arraignment of Error* (Morgan, PA: Soli Deo Gloria Publications, 1999; first published 1646 in London), is entirely dedicated to this thesis.

5

It's Not a Bloodsport

I choose to look at people through God, using God as
my glasses, colored with His love for them.

~ Frank Laubach

A careful read of church history will chill your blood. From the
late fourth century until the seventeenth century, Christians
slaughtered their fellow brethren over doctrinal differences.[1]

Sure, there were doctrinal wars undertaken in print where
one writer would quarrel at pen's point with another author.
However, the pamphlet wars eventually evolved into something far worse.

Christian leaders began unsheathing their swords and the
bloodletting began. Tragically, the blood has been flowing
ever since, even today in the West where there is freedom of
religion (I'm speaking metaphorically).

During the past four decades, I've been given a front-row seat to watch a number of church splits. In every case, it began with someone getting their feelings hurt and going on the warpath.

I remember one case in particular. A man came into our fellowship with a pet doctrine that he wanted everyone else to embrace. (We'll call him Tom.) Tom was so persistent he could wear down a granite mountain. He ran our blood hot.

Despite his efforts, we didn't accept Tom's teaching. He got his feelings hurt and the Ginsu knife made its appearance.

Someone decided to throw a match into the situation by correcting Tom. The result: we could all smell flesh burning. Others tried to correct Tom too, but they were left sucking air. Tom became so angry, he had smoke blowing out of both ears. (I'm aging by the moment as I think about it.)

Tom exploded into criticism and began vilifying the members of the church, accusing them of despicable and heinous things—none of which were true. He was on full meltdown, spewing venom wherever he could. Beyond his blistering denunciations, his sentiment was, "I wash my hands of those people!"

The words of judo champion Dumitru D. Coman come to mind: "When a toxic person can no longer control you, they will try to control how others see you."

Regrettably, I've watched this same drama play out in different settings. Different actors, but the same scenes packed with the same slurs.

The lesson is a chilling one. If you're going to meet in close quarters with other Christians, put your asbestos suit on. Someone is going to unleash toxins. And it will be over either a personality conflict or a doctrinal difference. (Often, these two are joined at the hip.)

More ironic, they will use the name of God and "protecting others" as a justification to malign their sisters and brothers in Christ. (Historically, those who incinerated heretics by fire or tortured them have always used "God's name" and the "protection of the sheep" as their defense.)

The blood that flowed at the hands of Christians over theological disagreements in the sixteenth century was up to the horse's bit. The tragic endings of John Huss, William Tyndale, Felix Manz, Balthasar Hubmaier, and countless Anabaptists will curdle your blood.

But we've come a long way today. We've come two millimeters!

Christians who have thin hide may not use the sword to impale those with whom they disagree. They'll use the keyboard and the internet instead. But the effect is the same—*carnage*.

Throughout this book, I'm going to declare holy war on this entire attitude. Treating our fellow brethren with the love of Jesus Christ is written in the very bloodstream of God. And you can find it all over the New Testament.

To put it another way, theology doesn't have to be a bloodsport. It can be a civil and intellectually honest conversation.

And it should be.

Unfortunately, much of the problem today is that Christians use different *conversational styles* when they discuss theology.* So the disagreement ends up being rooted in semantics rather than in substance. This isn't always the case, of course. But it happens more than you'd expect.

Yet it should not be so among God's people.

---

*In *Revise Us Again*, I identify the three different spiritual conversational styles and give tips on how to recognize and overcome each of them.

6

The Shocking Beliefs of C. S. Lewis

People pour themselves into their own doctrines, and
God has to blast them out of their preconceived ideas
before they can become devoted to Jesus Christ.

~ Oswald Chambers

With the popularity of his Chronicles of Narnia (selling millions), *Mere Christianity*, and *The Screwtape Letters* (both considered classics among evangelicals), Clive Staples Lewis is regarded by many to be a saint of evangelicalism.[1]

Christianity Today even called him "our patron saint."[2]

According to *Time* magazine, Lewis was "one of the most influential spokesmen for Christianity in the English-speaking world."[3]

According to J. I. Packer, Lewis was "a Christ-centered, great-tradition mainstream Christian whose stature a generation after his death seems greater than anyone ever thought while he was alive, and whose Christian writings are now seen as having classic status."[4]

An erstwhile atheist, Lewis converted to Christianity and quickly became a renowned defender of the faith and an evangelical paragon. Lewis converted in 1931. His BBC lectures from 1942 to 1944 eventually became his book *Mere Christianity* (1952), establishing him as a renowned defender.

Interestingly, Lewis died the same day that John F. Kennedy did—November 22, 1963.[5]

Not a good day for anyone to die. Many people didn't hear about Lewis's death until months later. All the oxygen was taken up covering Kennedy's tragic death.

Here are a few highlights about Lewis's life:

- He gave away a good portion of his royalties from his Christian books to those in need. This rendered him poor during his lifetime.[6]
- He had a near photographic memory.[7]
- While he was brilliant, he was also awkward and clumsy. He never learned to drive an automobile or use a typewriter.[8]
- He was intentional to craft handwritten responses to everyone who wrote him.[9]
- He fought in World War I and engaged in "trench warfare."[10]
- Later in his life, he felt that his intellectual powers for defending the gospel had worn thin. Consequently, he felt that he was a failure as an apologist because he couldn't persuade his closest friends and loved ones to accept the gospel.[11]

- In his *Problem of Pain*, Lewis employed unassailable logic in unveiling God's goodness and the problem of evil in the world. But when his wife passed away, he felt his earlier arguments about evil and pain were no longer adequate. His upgraded thinking on the subject appears in his later work, *A Grief Observed*.[12]

Yet despite his amazing contribution to the Christian faith, here are seven shocking beliefs that Lewis held.

1. Lewis believed in praying for the dead.

Here's a quote:

> Of course I pray for the dead. The action is so spontaneous, so all but inevitable, that only the most compulsive theological case against it would deter me. And I hardly know how the rest of my prayers would survive if those for the dead were forbidden.[13]

2. Lewis believed in purgatory.

Springing out of his belief of praying for the dead was his belief in purgatorial cleansing. According to Roman Catholic dogma, purgatory is the final purification of the elect after death.[14]

In *A Grief Observed*, Lewis talked about his deceased wife, Joy, connecting her to suffering and cleansing in purgatory.

Lewis believed in salvation by grace, but he thought complete transformation was dependent upon one's choice. Thus he felt that transformation can even occur after death, and some Christians need to be cleansed in order to be fit for heaven and enjoy it.

For Lewis, purgatory was designed to create complete sanctification, not retribution or punishment. So Lewis saw purgatory as a work of grace.

Here are some revealing quotes from Lewis:

> To pray [for the dead] presupposes that progress and difficulty are still possible. In fact, you are bringing in something like Purgatory.
>
> Well, I suppose that I am. Though even in Heaven some perpetual increase of beatitude, reached by a continually more ecstatic self-surrender, without the possibility of failure but not perhaps without its own ardours and exertions—for delight also has its severities and steep ascents, as lovers know—might be supposed. But I won't press, or guess, that side for the moment. I believe in Purgatory.[15]

3. Lewis believed that it was possible for some unbelievers to find salvation after they have left this world.

While Lewis didn't subscribe to universalism or ultimate reconciliation, he did believe that salvation after death was a possibility for some.

His view was that some people may seek and find Christ without knowing Him by name. However, he was very clear that this was not "salvation by sincerity" or "goodness" but rather a Spirit-driven desire for God.[16]

For Lewis, Christianity is not the only revelation of God's way, but it is the complete and perfect revelation. Lewis, therefore, didn't hold to the idea that all roads lead equally to God. In addition, Lewis believed that time may not work the same way after death as it does in life. Thus all those who lived before Christ and after might be subject to the grace of repentance.[17]

Interestingly, Lewis's distant mentor, George MacDonald, believed in ultimate reconciliation (meaning, hell will be empty because God will win everyone to Himself in the end). Lewis's regard for MacDonald was incomparable.

He said of MacDonald, "I dare not say that he is never in error; but to speak plainly I know hardly any other writer who seems to be closer, or more continually close, to the Spirit of Christ Himself."[18]

That's quite a statement to make about someone you don't fully agree with doctrinally.

4. Lewis believed that it was acceptable for Christians to drink alcohol.

In contrast, many evangelicals today believe that all Christians should abstain from alcohol. Here's a direct quote by Lewis on this point:

> Temperance is, unfortunately, one of those words that has changed its meaning. It now usually means teetotalism. . . . It is a mistake to think that Christians ought to be teetotalers; Mohammedanism, not Christianity, is the teetotal religion.[19]

5. Lewis believed that the book of Job wasn't historical and that the Bible contained errors.

This view will be shocking to some evangelicals, especially the conservative wing, since Lewis is widely regarded as an evangelical icon.

> The *Book of Job* appears to me unhistorical because it begins about a man quite unconnected with all history or even legend, with no genealogy, living in a country of which the Bible elsewhere has hardly anything to say; because, in fact, the author quite obviously writes as a story-teller not as a chronicler.[20]

> The human qualities of the raw materials [of the Bible] show through. Naïvety, error, contradiction, even (as in the cursing Psalms) wickedness are not removed. The total result is not "the Word of God" in the sense that every passage, in itself, gives impeccable science or history. It carries the Word of God.[21]

6. Lewis didn't believe that all parts of the Bible were the Word of God.

In his *Reflections on the Psalms*, Lewis made these interesting comments:

> Speaking of judgment and hatred in the Psalms. [Lewis calls them, "the vindictive Psalms, the cursings"; they are also known as "the imprecatory Psalms."] Yet there must be some Christian use to be made of them; if, at least we [Christians] still believe (as I do) that all Holy Scripture is in some sense— though not all parts of it in the same sense—the word of God.[22]

7. Lewis believed that the creation account in Genesis may have been derived from pagan sources.

Here's a quote:

> I have therefore no difficulty in accepting, say, the view of those scholars who tell us that the account of Creation in

Genesis is derived from earlier Semitic stories which were Pagan and mythical.[23]

In closing, J. I. Packer—a man many consider to be a pillar of midcentury evangelicalism—sums up the shocking beliefs of C. S. Lewis this way:

> By ordinary evangelical standards, his idea about the Atonement (archetypal penitence, rather than penal substitution), and his failure to ever mention justification by faith when speaking of the forgiveness of sins, and his apparent hospitality to baptismal regeneration, and his noninerrantist view of biblical inspiration, plus his quiet affirmation of purgatory and of the possible final salvation of some who have left this world as nonbelievers, were weaknesses; they led the late, great, Martyn Lloyd Jones, for whom evangelical orthodoxy was mandatory, to doubt whether Lewis was a Christian at all.[24]

Yet despite Lewis's "shocking views" on various matters, Packer commends him:

> The combination within him of insight with vitality, wisdom with wit, imaginative power with analytical precision made Lewis a sparkling communicator of the everlasting gospel. . . .
> Long may we learn from the contents of his marvelous, magical mind! I doubt whether the full measure of him has been taken by anyone as yet.[25]

So if you happen to be a Lewis fan, I hope this chapter will encourage you to extend some extra grace to the next person with whom you disagree over doctrine.

Let's now turn our attention to another great Christian who shaped church history.

7

The Shocking Beliefs
of Jonathan Edwards

It takes God a long time to get us to stop thinking that
unless everyone sees things exactly as we do, they must
be wrong. That is never God's view.

~ Oswald Chambers

Jonathan Edwards is a legend—a hero to many. Although the
Yale-educated Calvinist theologian/philosopher lived in the
eighteenth century, many who embrace Reformed theology
give Edwards rock-star status.

The ubiquitous "Jonathan Edwards is my homeboy" T-
shirts and coffee mugs are glaring examples. (I'm sorry, but
neither the publisher nor I will be selling those.)

Historians regard Edwards to be *the* theologian of the First
Great Awakening (while George Whitefield was its promoter).[1]

The respected Lutheran theologian Robert Jenson dubbed
Edwards "America's Theologian."[2]

The body of theological works Edwards produced in his day—without computers or voice-activation software—is stunning and formidable. More startling, Edwards completed a vast amount of work in a short period. He died at the young age of fifty-five from an experimental smallpox vaccination.

According to his daughter, Edwards spent thirteen hours a day in his study. And by his own admission, he once said of himself, "I am fitted for no other business but study."[3]

Yet beyond Edwards's uncanny mental abilities and introverted personality, a little-known fact is that he was a strong advocate for Native American rights.

He was bitterly critical when New Englanders had stolen land from Native Americans. It was his desire that they pay for the land they took.[4]

So Edwards—the logical Reformed personality—became a "social activist" engaged in "social justice." This is interesting since many contemporary Edwards followers eschew social activism and social justice.

Even so, some American Christians venerate Edwards with almost cultlike regard. Thus any critique of his views is taken by some to be on a par with blaspheming the Holy Spirit.

So let me be clear: *I, Frank Viola, believe that Jonathan Edwards was an incredible man whom God greatly used.*

(If you're a die-hard Edwards fan, reread that sentence please.)

Every Westerner who paid attention in history class knows Edwards from his infamous sermon, "Sinners in the Hands of an Angry God."

What's fascinating about this is that, according to the historical accounts, Edwards didn't preach that sermon, he read it, as was his usual custom. And he wasn't yelling when he did.[5]

In light of that introduction, the following views held by Edwards will be met with either shock or surprise by many Christians today.

1. Edwards believed that being a slave owner was not incompatible with being a follower of Jesus.

While Edwards was an advocate of Native American rights and denounced the transatlantic slave trade, he himself was a slave owner. Granted, Edwards believed that all humans were created equal by God and that slaves should be treated with respect.[6]

Many, if not most, of today's evangelicals view slavery to be among the greatest evils in history. For "America's greatest theologian" to own slaves is, well, shocking, even if he was simply acting in accordance with the times. Edwards was part of the aristocratic elite stratum of his society.

As one writer put it,

> To expect Edwards to oppose slavery amidst the conflicts with the French and Native Americans would be akin to expecting soldiers to contribute to cancer research during a world war. It would be a good thing to do, but it probably wouldn't rank among the most pressing concerns to the soldier. So it was with Edwards. Edwards the man was inescapably a man of his time—an aristocratic, revival focused, British patriot. Those were his blinders.[7]

This point sobers popular notions that Edwards always interpreted Scripture correctly, when in reality, he was influenced by the culture of his day in his understanding of Scripture. The fact that one of America's greatest theologians owned slaves is a testament to the fact that no human—however great they may be—sees every angle of everything.

2. Edwards believed that the office of the papacy was the Antichrist.

Apologies to the Roman Catholic Church, but despite his impressive mental acumen, Edwards actually believed this. While a number of conservative evangelicals have been raised on this idea, most evangelical and mainstream Christians find it aberrant.

One writer states, "Edwards concluded that we can be certain that the Antichrist had embodied himself in the Roman Papacy."[8]

3. Edwards believed that God hates sinners worse than you hate poison.

Edwards used intense imagery of eternally suffering in hell as a form of evangelism.

By contrast, many evangelical preachers today use more "polite" methods of evangelism, including appeals to become a Christian so one can reach their maximum potential.

Edwards's description of painful eternal torment will be shocking to many modern Christians.

This is from his "Sinners in the Hands of an Angry God" sermon:

> The God that holds you over the pit of hell, much as one holds a spider, or some loathsome insect, over the fire, abhors you,

and is dreadfully provoked; his wrath towards you burns like fire; he looks upon you as worthy of nothing else, but to be cast into the fire; he is of purer eyes than to bear to have you in his sight; you are ten thousand times so abominable in his eyes, as the most hateful venomous serpent is in ours. You have offended him infinitely more than ever a stubborn rebel did his prince: and yet it is nothing but his hand that holds you from falling into the fire every moment: it is ascribed to nothing else, that you did not go to hell the last night; that you was suffered to awake again in this world, after you closed your eyes to sleep; and there is no other reason to be given, why you have not dropped into hell since you arose in the morning, but that God's hand has held you up: there is no other reason to be given why you have not gone to hell, since you have sat here in the house of God, provoking his pure eyes by your sinful wicked manner of attending his solemn worship: yea, there is nothing else that is to be given as a reason why you do not this very moment drop down into hell.[9]

Whether you agree with this piece of prose or not, the ideas—and the language—are a first-class shocker for most modern Christians.[10]

4. Edwards believed that the revivals happening in the 1740s were "the dawning" or "prelude" of the consummation of the ages where "the world would be renewed," and that God's great and last work on the earth *began* in America.

Here's a direct quote:

It is not unlikely that this work of God's Spirit, so extraordinary and wonderful, is the dawning, or, at least, a prelude of that glorious work of God, so often foretold in Scripture, which, in the progress and issue of it, shall renew the world of mankind. If we consider how long since the things foretold as what should precede this great event, have been accomplished; and how long this event has been expected by the church of God, and thought to be nigh by the most eminent men of God in the church; and withal consider what the state of things now is, and has for a considerable time been, in the church of God, and the world of mankind; we cannot reasonably think otherwise, than that the beginning of this great work of God must be near. And there are many things that make it probable that this work will begin in America.[11]

Christians in many countries have believed that the Lord has destined *their country* to be the place where God's last and final work on the earth would begin and spread.

Edwards was a postmillennialist, thus he expected a golden age. This is in contrast with the myriad of Christians who are looking at the state of America and expecting the rapture at any moment due to the godless state of the world.

When looking at America since the days of Edwards—even up until today—a case can be made that his prediction of the "dawning" or "prelude" of the "glorious work of God as foretold by Scripture" in America was simply wrong.[12]

5. Edwards believed that emotional outbursts that included bodily manifestations were normative during a revival.

I remember when the Toronto Blessing hit North America in the mid-1990s. Many fundamentalists, evangelicals, and Reformed Christians came against it with switchblades and hand grenades, condemning the movement because of the emotional outbursts.

Interestingly, those who were leading the "blessing" pointed to the writings of Jonathan Edwards to justify that these manifestations were marks of real revival. And, well, whether you believe that the so-called Toronto Blessing was a work of God, a work of the devil, or the work of hand-waving magicians, they had a point.

Edwards may not have said grace over everything that occurred in the mid-1990s (some of it started to escalate into the bizarre). But one thing is clear. In 1734, people began responding to Edwards's sermons with emotional outbursts and even the loss of bodily strength. They also testified to remarkable changes in their lives, just as those who "got the blessing" in the mid-1990s did.[13]

So the big point here is that Edwards saw emotional outbursts and other bodily phenomenon as a mark of revival. (He explained that this was a human response in some people to the power of the Spirit.)[14]

6. Edwards believed that mystical experiences were part of the Christian experience.

Some of you who are reading that statement may be having apoplexy right now. Let me define what I mean by "mystical." That word has been used to either damn people or dignify them.

By "mystical," I mean an experience that is spiritual and goes beyond the faculties of the frontal lobe. In describing the following entry by Edwards, the historian Henry Sheldon says that "he was transported by a species of ecstasy by contemplation of divine verities."[15]

Edwards describes an experience he had with words like "view," "appeared," and "sense." But he wasn't talking about seeing with the physical eye or sensing with the physical senses. He was rather talking about a spiritual "seeing" and a spiritual "sensing."

On one occasion, the "vision"—or spiritual seeing—caused him to weep aloud for almost a full hour. Edwards pointed out that he had experiences like this numerous times. I've italicized the mystical terms in this quote of his below.

> I had a *view* that for me was extraordinary, of the glory of the Son of God, as Mediator between God and man, and his wonderful, great, full, pure and sweet grace and love, and meek and gentle condescension. This grace that *appeared* so calm and sweet, *appeared* also great above the heavens. The person of Christ *appeared* ineffably excellent with an excellency great enough to swallow up all thought and conception—which continued, as near as I can judge, *about an hour*; which kept me the greater part of the time in *a flood of tears, and weeping aloud*. I *felt* an ardency of soul to be, what I know not otherwise how to express, emptied and annihilated; to lie in the dust, and to be full of Christ alone; to love him with a holy and pure love; to trust in him; to live upon him; to serve and follow him; and to be perfectly sanctified and made pure, with a divine and heavenly purity. *I have, several other times, had views very much of the same nature, and which have had the same effects.*[16]

Whether you like it or not, this is all mystical language. What makes this "shocking" is that I've never met an admirer of Edwards who described a personal spiritual experience like this, unless they were charismatic Calvinists.

But I've met many Edwards admirers who regarded such experiences—when described by others—as being the mark of a "Cereal Christian" (a flake, fruit, or nut).

7. Edwards believed that God's sovereignty requires that He create the entire universe out of nothing at every moment.

On this point, theologian Roger Olson writes,

> Edwards argued that God's sovereignty requires that he create the entire universe and everything in it ex nihilo at every moment. That goes far beyond garden variety creation ex nihilo or continuous creation. It is speculative and dangerous. He also asserted that God is space itself. And he came very close to denying that God's creation of the world was free in any libertarian sense as if God could have done otherwise. (He said that God always does what is most wise, something with which few Christians would argue, but somehow one must admit the possibility that God might not have created at all. Otherwise the world becomes necessary even for God which undermines grace.)[17]

8. Edwards believed that Arminianism was a slippery slope toward atheism.

Throughout my life, I've met a handful of Christians who believed that Arminians shouldn't be allowed near small children or pets. Edwards may not have held that view, but he did believe that Arminianism was not only false, but dangerous. On this point Roger Olson states,

Edwards considered Arminianism of any kind—even Wesley's warm-hearted, evangelical Arminian theology—an implicit denial of God's greatness and a step down the slippery slope toward atheism.[18]

In closing, did I tell you that I believe Jonathan Edwards was a great man whom God greatly used?

Let's regrace!

In the next chapter, we'll examine the shocking beliefs of the individual who is credited with founding Protestant Christianity.

8

The Shocking Beliefs of Martin Luther

The knowledge that God has loved me beyond all limits will compel me to go into the world to love others in the same way. I may get irritated because I have to live with an unusually difficult person. But just think how disagreeable I have been with God! Am I prepared to be identified so closely with the Lord Jesus that His life and His sweetness will be continually poured out through Me?

~ Oswald Chambers

For many Christians, Martin Luther is a household name. He was a monumental reformer—touted as the father of the Protestant Reformation.

Almost three hundred years after Luther's passing, Ralph Waldo Emerson said of him, "Martin Luther the reformer is one of the most extraordinary persons in history and has left a deeper impression of his presence in the modern world than any other except Columbus."[1]

While in his early twenties, Luther became an Augustinian monk. But he wore himself out with prayer, fasting, and excessive confessions, trying to earn God's favor.

Later, he had a revelation of God's grace and justification by faith (alone) while reading the book of Romans. (His revelation is alleged to have come to him while he was sitting on the toilet. But this story has been debunked.)[2]

Luther's reformation began when he started opposing a man named John Tetzel who was selling indulgences to raise money to finance the building of St. Peter's Cathedral. Luther was against the abuse of indulgences, believing it to be a perversion of the gospel. So in reaction, he wrote his famed Ninety-Five Theses.

It's commonly held that Luther nailed his Ninety-Five Theses on the door of the castle church in Wittenberg, inviting scholars to debate the issue. But some historians doubt that he actually posted the theses on the door at all.[3]

Nevertheless, with the advent of the printing press, Luther's Ninety-Five Theses were printed and distributed widely.

Luther was rebuked by the leadership of the Roman Catholic Church and given space to recant and repent. Luther refused, however. As a result, he was condemned by the Church, branded a heretic, excommunicated, banished, and condemned by the emperor.

He was to be captured and killed on sight. But Luther survived because he was kidnapped and protected by Frederick III, Elector of Saxony ("Frederick the Wise").

Luther translated the New Testament into German so that the common people could understand it. There are approximately 60,000 pages of text attributed to Luther. Yet he apparently wished "all my books would disappear and the Holy Scriptures alone would be read."[4]

During much of his life, Luther was subjected to a barrage of slander and rumor. One of these rumors was that he was the offspring of his mother and the devil.[5]

Cartoons were made of him, shaming, blaming, and condemning him. One of them depicted him as a seven-headed monster. His response to it was, "A cartoon has appeared of me as a monster with seven heads. I must be invincible, because they cannot overcome me when I only have one."[6]

In 1525, Luther married a runaway nun who was sixteen years his junior. Her name was Katharina von Bora.

Luther felt that beer and wine were God's gifts. He possessed a mug with three rings on it—the first ring represented the Ten Commandments, the second represented the Apostles' Creed, and the third represented the Lord's Prayer.[7]

There's no doubt that Luther recovered some wonderful truths that were lost to the body of Christ. He stood as a prophet against a corrupt Church. He restored the great doctrine of justification by faith, freeing God's people from legalism and the need to go through human mediators to get to God. He gave the Bible back to God's people. He also had a strong hand in restoring music and singing to the body of Christ.[8]

Before you read on, keep the following in mind:

Luther lived in the sixteenth century. Life was cruel and harsh, and people were generally violent. To bring this point home, imagine this scenario. Suppose that Christians two hundred years from now discover that some of the items we use on a daily basis were destroying the planet. So they may think, *How could those Christians in the twenty-first century be so selfish and sinful!?* Again, we have to understand Luther, Calvin, and others against the times in which they lived.

Repeat: The point of this chapter—and this book—is *not* for you to conclude, "Oh my, these guys were horrible. Put them on the chopping block!" It's the opposite. If the great theologians who shaped evangelical Christianity could be so right on some things, and so off on others, then certainly we need to be more tolerant, civil, and gracious with our fellow brethren today when we disagree.

With that said, what follows are some of the shocking beliefs of the great Protestant Reformer, Martin Luther.

1. Luther despised Jewish people, believing that they deserved persecution.

At first, Luther was sympathetic to the Jews and critical of Roman Catholics for their mistreatment of the Jews, for "treating them like dogs" and thus making it difficult for them to come to Jesus Christ.[9]

But fifteen years later, he changed his tune entirely and began to excoriate the Jewish people in his writings.[10]

Despite the fact that Luther's best friends disapproved of his contra-Jewish attacks, he wouldn't relent. In fact, shortly before his death, Luther wrote, "We are at fault for not slaying them!"[11]

Church historian Roland Bainton wrote that it would probably have been better if Luther had died before he wrote his onslaught against the Jews.[12]

In his *On the Jews and Their Lies*, Luther stated,

I advise that their houses also be razed and destroyed, . . . I advise that all their prayer books and Talmudic writings, in which such idolatry, lies, cursing, and blasphemy are taught, be taken from them. . . . I advise that their rabbis be forbidden to teach henceforth on pain of loss of life and limb. . . . I advise that safe-conduct on the highways be abolished completely for the Jews. . . . I advise that usury be prohibited to them, and that all cash and treasure of silver and gold be taken from them and put aside for safekeeping. . . . If this does not help we must drive them out like mad dogs, so that we do not become partakers of their abominable blasphemy and all their other vices and thus merit God's wrath and be damned with them.[13]

And again,

In sum, they are the Devil's children, damned to hell. If there is anything human left in them, for that one this treatise might be useful. One can hope for the whole bunch as one wills, but I have no hope. I also know no biblical text [that supports such hope].[14]

Note that Luther's issue with the Jews didn't appear to be racial, but theological.[15]

Luther was frustrated that they rejected Jesus, and he couldn't convince them otherwise. On this score, he wrote,

Just as I may eat, drink, sleep, walk, ride with, buy from, speak to, and deal with a heathen, Jew, Turk, or heretic, so I may also marry and continue in wedlock with him. Pay no attention to the precepts of those fools who forbid it. . . . A heathen is just as much a man or a woman—God's good creation—as St. Peter, St. Paul, and St. Lucy.[16]

Luther also opposed the Jews because of his historicist eschatology, which viewed the Turks, the Pope, and the Jews as part of a great end-time coalition designed to wipe out Christians under the leadership of the devil.[17]

2. Luther held to several shocking views about marriage and sex.

Here are some examples:

> When one resists the other and refuses the conjugal duty she is robbing the other of the body she had bestowed upon him. This is really contrary to marriage, and dissolves the marriage. For this reason the civil government must compel the wife, or put her to death. If the government fails to act, the husband must reason that his wife has been stolen away and slain by robbers; he must seek another. We would certainly have to accept it if someone's life were taken from him. Why then should we not also accept it if a wife steals herself away from her husband, or is stolen away by others?[18]

> As to divorce, it is still a question for debate whether it is allowable. For my part I so greatly detest divorce that I should prefer bigamy to it; but whether it is allowable, I do not venture to decide.[19]

> For my part, I confess that I do not see how I can prevent polygamy; there is not in the sacred texts the least word against those who take several wives at one time; but there are many things permissible that ought not becomingly to be done: of these is bigamy.[20]

3. Luther denied the canonicity of the books of Hebrews, James, Jude, and Revelation.

He did so for two reasons. One reason is that he believed these books went against the Protestant doctrines such as *sola gratia* (by grace alone) and *sola fide* (by faith alone). The other reason is because these books had their canonicity questioned by others.[21]

In his preface to the New Testament, Luther ascribed to several books of the New Testament different degrees of doctrinal value, saying,

> In a word St. John's Gospel and his first epistle, St. Paul's epistles, especially Romans, Galatians, and Ephesians, and St. Peter's first epistle are the books that show you Christ and teach you all that is necessary and salvatory for you to know, even if you were never to see or hear any other book or doctrine. Therefore St. James' epistle is really an epistle of straw, compared to these others, for it has nothing of the nature of the gospel about it. But more of this in the other prefaces.[22]

In another place, he wrote,

> Though this epistle of St. James was rejected by the ancients, I praise it and consider it a good book, because it sets up no doctrines of men but vigorously promulgates the law of God. However, to state my own opinion about it, though without prejudice to anyone, I do not regard it as the writing of an apostle.[23]

4. Luther believed it was justified—and even divinely ordered—that civil disobedience be punished severely, as demonstrated in the Peasants' War.

In the beginning, Luther stood on the side of the peasants. He made this plain in his *Admonition to Peace*. In it, he blamed the conflict on the rulers. His view was that the rulers should oblige the peasants.

But after he observed the unruly behavior of the peasants, he changed his position. In his treatise *Against the Robbing and Murdering Hordes of Peasants*, Luther urged the princes with these words:

> Furthermore, anyone who can be proved to be a seditious person is an outlaw before God and the emperor; and whoever is the first to put him to death does right and well. For if a man is in open rebellion, everyone is both his judge and his executioner; just as when a fire starts, the first man who can put it out is the best man to do the job. For rebellion is not just simple murder; it is like a great fire, which attacks and devastates a whole land. Thus rebellion brings with it a land filled with murder and bloodshed; it makes widows and orphans, and turns everything upside down, like the worst disaster. Therefore let everyone who can, smite, slay, and stab, secretly or openly, remembering that nothing can be more poisonous, hurtful, or devilish than a rebel. It is just as when one must kill a mad dog; if you do not strike him, he will strike you, and a whole land with you.[24]

On this score, historian H. A. L. Fisher wrote,

> The manner in which he [Luther] dissociated his movement from the peasant rebellion . . . and the encouragement he

gave to a course of repression so savage that it left the German peasantry more defenseless and abased than any social class in central or western Europe, are serious blots upon his good name. The German peasants were rough men and rough fighters; but their grievances were genuine, and their original demands were just and reasonable.[25]

Here are some other quotes by Luther on the matter:

> The wise man says, "Cibus, onus et virga asino;" "straw for the peasant." They have gone mad and will not hear the Word, and so they must bear the rod, that is, the guns; it serves them right. We ought to pray for them that they may be obedient; if not, then let the shot whistle, or they will make things a thousandfold worse.[26]

> Preachers are the greatest murderers because they admonish the ruler to do his duty and punish the guilty. I, Martin Luther, slew all the peasants in the uprising, for I ordered that they be put to death; all their blood is on my neck. But I refer it all to our Lord God, who commanded me to speak as I did. The devil and the ungodly kill, but they have no right to. Accordingly priests and official persons must be distinguished well, so that we may see that magistrates can condemn by law and can put to death by virtue of their office. Today, by the grace of God, they have learned this well. Now they abuse their power against the gospel, but they won't get fat from it.[27]

5. Luther believed that heretics should be put to death.

By 1530, Luther believed that blasphemy was punishable by death, and he included "false teaching" in that definition.[28]

In 1536, Philip Melanchthon drafted a memorandum demanding death for all Anabaptists, and Luther signed it.[29]

6. Luther believed that writing in anger, using profanity, and shaming his enemies by name-calling was justified.

If you ever got on Luther's bad side, you'd be wise to run for cover.

Note his words:

> Anger refreshes all my blood, sharpens my mind, and drives away temptations. . . . I was born to war with fanatics and devils. Thus my books are very stormy and bellicose.[30]

Church history buffs are well aware of Luther's unkind and coarse tone as well as his penchant to be angry and bullheaded. In addition, name-calling wasn't beneath him. On this score, Luther wrote,

> I cannot deny that I am more vehement than I should be. . . . But they assail me and God's Word so atrociously and criminally that . . . these monsters are carrying me beyond the bounds of moderation.[31]

And again,

> We should take him—the pope, the cardinals, and whatever riffraff belongs to His Idolatrous and Papal Holiness—and (as blasphemers) tear out their tongues from the back, and nail them on the gallows in the order in which they hang their seals on the bulls, even though all this is mild compared to their blasphemy and idolatry.[32]

Luther believed that using profanity was acceptable. For example, he called the Jewish rabbi's interpretation of Scripture "Jewish piss and shi*."[33]

He reprimanded his Catholic opponents, saying, "How often do I have to yell at you, you crude and unlearned papists, before you come with Scripture at least once? Scripture, Scripture, Scripture! Don't you hear me, you dumb goat and crude ass?"[34]

In this regard, Erasmus is purported to have said of Luther, "God has sent in this latter age a violent physician on account of the magnitude of the existing disorders."[35]

Luther is purported to have once declared,

> I wrote it after dining—but a Christian can speak better inebriated than a papist can sober.[36]

Luther's collaborator, Melanchthon, admitted that he could "neither deny, nor excuse, or praise" Luther's coarse writings.[37]

On balance, scattered references and crude language would only amount to a couple of pages total in his numerous books.[38]

7. Luther believed that all physical ailments were the work of Satan.

Luther's view was that sickness and disease were used by the devil to persuade believers to forsake Jesus. He strongly approved of doctors, even though they didn't realize that the cause of sickness was the devil.[39]

8. Luther ridiculed and disparaged some of his opponents in the Reformation.

Luther often clashed with his fellow Protestant Reformers. Andreas Karlstadt was a professor at the university of Wittenberg who promoted Luther to the doctorate in 1512. But both men had a heated exchange at the Black Bear Tavern. And thus began a bloodletting doctrinal war between the two men.

In one of his publications, Luther ridiculed Karlstadt. Theirs was largely a dispute over the Lord's Supper, disagreeing over the meaning of the words "this is my body."

In Luther's eyes, Karlstadt and the Swiss Reformer Zwingli were "willful liars," "sect leaders," and "novices in the Scriptures."[40]

Luther once disparaged Zwingli, saying, "I have bitten into many a nut, believing it to be good, only to find it wormy. Zwingli and Erasmus are nothing but wormy nuts that taste like crap in one's mouth!"[41]

The bad blood between Luther and other Reformers set an example of uncivil dialogue and noncooperation between Protestant leaders that continues to this day.

Luther's vehemence was even greater toward the Anabaptists. He castigated them as "fanatics" and a "seditious mob."[42]

In 1532, Luther commented, "So the Anabaptists reject baptism almost entirely. The pope, who distorts it, nevertheless allows baptism to remain."[43]

———

Two closing historical notes for those who are interested in the origins of modern church practices. These aren't "shocking" beliefs, just interesting points of history.

(1) Luther didn't use the word priest to refer to the new clergy of the Reformation, but the ministry was essentially the same.

He wrote,

> We neither can nor ought to give the name priest to those who are in charge of the Word and sacrament among the people. The reason they have been called priests is either because of the custom of the heathen people or as a vestige of the Jewish nation. The result is greatly injurious to the church.[44]

Yet as I pointed out in my book *Pagan Christianity*, not much changed between the Catholic priest and the Protestant pastor during the Reformation. The "priest" was transformed into the "preacher," "the minister," and finally "the pastor."

Catholic priests had seven duties at the time of the Reformation: preaching; the sacraments; prayers for the flock; a disciplined, godly life; church rites; supporting the poor; and visiting the sick. The Protestant pastor took upon himself all of these responsibilities—plus he sometimes blessed civic events.

The famed poet John Milton summed the idea up by saying, "New presbyter is but old priest writ large."[45]

In other words, because of the way Luther viewed and wrote about the priests and the new ministers of the Reformation, identifying the latter as responsible for the same rites as Roman Catholic priests, Luther held that the Protestant pastor was little more than a priest with a new title.

(2) Luther detested the word "church" as a translation for ekklesia.

The renowned theologian Emil Brunner wrote about this point, saying,

> Of all the great teachers of Christianity, Martin Luther perceived most clearly the difference between the *Ecclesia* of the New Testament and the institutional church, and reacted most sharply against the *quid pro quo* which would identify them. Therefore he refused to tolerate the mere word "church": he called it an "obscure ambiguous" term (7). In his translation of the Bible, he rendered the New Testament *"Ecclesia"* by "congregation." . . . He realized that the New Testament *Ecclesia* is just not an "it", "a thing", an "institution", but rather a unity of persons, a people, a communion. . . .
>
> Strong as was Luther's aversion to the word "church", the facts of history prove stronger. The linguistic usage of both the Reformation and the post-Reformation era had to come to terms with the so powerfully developed idea of the Church, and consequently all the confusion dependent upon the use of this "obscure ambiguous" word penetrated Reformation theology. It was impossible to put the clock back one millennium and a half. The conception "church" remained irrevocably moulded by this historical process of 1,500 years.[46]

I happen to agree with this sentiment, but it's an interesting, yet little-known fact about the great Reformer.

All told, if you're a Luther fan, I hope you will have a bit more grace when you meet a fellow Christian who you believe to be theologically wrong. For even the leader of the Protestant Reformation didn't see all things clearly.

Let's now turn our attention to one of the most influential Christian leaders of all time.

9

The Shocking Beliefs of John Calvin

Beware of anything that competes with your loyalty to
Jesus Christ. The greatest competitor of true devotion
to Jesus is the service we do for Him. It is easier to serve
than to pour out our lives completely for Him. The
goal of the call of God is His satisfaction, not simply
that we should do something for Him.

~ Oswald Chambers

John Calvin played a significant role in the development of
Reformed theology, a theology that still flourishes today.
Hailed as a master theologian, the French Reformer's writ-
ings still live and breathe in the twenty-first century.

Calvin was a second-generation Reformer (he was twenty-
six years younger than Martin Luther). Trained as a lawyer,
he possessed a keen analytical mind.

By all counts, Calvin was an intellectual. He wrote the original version of his famous *Institutes of the Christian Religion* when he was only twenty-seven years old, updating it throughout his life. (Some regard the *Institutes* to be the single most influential theological work in history.)

Sometime between 1530 and 1533, Calvin experienced a spiritual conversion and joined the Reformation in 1537.

Whether you agree with Calvin's theological system or not, there's no question that John Calvin made an indelible mark on today's Christianity, including many segments of evangelicalism.

And like all highly influential Christians, Calvin has been hailed and hammered, loved and loathed, adored and abhorred.

Consider these quotes, for example:

> Among all those who have been born of women, there has not risen a greater than John Calvin; no age, before him ever produced his equal, and no age afterwards has seen his rival. In theology, he stands alone, shining like a bright fixed star, while other leaders and teachers can only circle round him, at a great distance—as comets go streaming through space—with nothing like his glory or his permanence . . . the longer I live the clearer does it appear that John Calvin's system is the nearest to perfection.[1]
>
> ~ Charles Spurgeon

> Taking into account all his failings he must be reckoned as one of the greatest and best of men whom God raised up in the history of Christianity.[2]
>
> ~ Philip Schaff

The famous Calvin, whom we regard as the apostle of Geneva, raised himself up to the rank of Pope of the Protestants (*s'érigea en pape des Protestants*).[3]

~ Voltaire

According to Will Durant, Calvin "labored twelve to eighteen hours a day as preacher, administrator, professor of theology, superintendent of churches and schools, advisor to municipal courts, and regulator of public morals and church liturgy."[4]

Calvin died at age fifty-four. But he was incredibly productive during his short life. Prolific since his early twenties, Calvin preached an average of five sermons a week and wrote a commentary on nearly every book of the Bible.

What follows is not intended to debate the ethics or theological veracity of Calvin—including his system of theology which is still held dear by many. That being interpreted means, those of you who are wired to interpret anything but praise for John Calvin as equating to being "anti-Calvin," calm down.

Along with Calvin's admirers, there exists a loud and vocal group of "Calvin-haters." Often, those who stand against Calvin's theology think that personally attacking John Calvin is a means of discrediting the theological system of Calvinism, but it's not.

I have high regard for Mr. Calvin and his contribution, even though I don't agree with everything he believed. I suspect that when you finish this chapter, you'll agree that not all of Calvin's viewpoints were compatible with the teachings of Jesus. That fact alone should make us all more tolerant toward those with whom we disagree over doctrines.

1. Calvin believed that executing some unrepentant heretics was justifiable.

Keep in mind that during the sixteenth century, the church and the state were symbiotically combined. Severe heresy, then, was punishable by death. It was viewed as leading to both societal anarchy and eternal death. Most Christians of that day accepted the death penalty for heretics, except for the Anabaptists (but that's another story).

The best known example of this societally accepted belief is when Calvin consented to the execution of Michael Servetus, a man who denied the Trinity and infant baptism. Servetus denied that Jesus was the Son of God in the orthodox sense.[5]

Servetus burned for thirty minutes before he died. Why? Simply because of his theological views. (Well, it was actually because the fire was really hot, but you get what I'm saying.)[6]

John Calvin's supporters are quick to point out that the great Reformer didn't directly execute the man. And he even tried to persuade Servetus not to come to Geneva. Calvin also attempted to get Servetus to repent and sought for him to be granted a more humane execution (which was beheading instead of burning).

Even so, Calvin made this remark regarding Servetus, showing that he believed death for heresy was justified:

> But I am unwilling to pledge my word for his safety, for if he shall come [to Geneva], I shall never permit him to depart alive, provided my authority be of any avail.[7]

One notable remark by Calvin was, "I hope that Servetus will be condemned to death, but I desire that he should be spared the cruelty of the punishment [of fire]."[8]

Nine years after the execution, Calvin made this comment when answering his critic François Baudouin:

> Servetus suffered the penalty due his heresies, but was it by my will? Certainly his arrogance destroyed him not less than his impiety. And what crime was it of mine if our Council, at my exhortation, indeed, but in conformity with the opinion of several Churches, took vengeance on his execrable blasphemies?
>
> Let Baudouin abuse me as long as he will, provided that, by the judgment of Melanchthon, posterity owes me a debt of gratitude for having purged the Church of so pernicious a monster.[9]

Calvin is also quoted as saying,

> Whoever shall now contend that it is unjust to put heretics and blasphemers to death will knowingly and willingly incur their very guilt. This is not laid down on human authority; it is God who speaks and prescribes a perpetual rule for his Church.[10]

One of Calvin's contemporaries, Sebastian Castellio, allegedly said this about him:

> If Christ himself came to Geneva, he would be crucified. For Geneva is not a place of Christian liberty. It is ruled by a new pope [referring to Calvin], but one who burns men alive while the pope at Rome at least strangles them first.[11]

Summarizing Castellio's feelings toward Calvin, Durant remarks,

> Can we imagine Christ ordering a man to be burned alive for advocating adult baptism? The Mosaic laws calling for

the death of a heretic were superceded by the law of Christ, which is one of mercy not of despotism and terror.[12]

Whether you agree with Calvin's view or defend his actions because he was "a man of his times," many Christians today find the idea of executing heretics to be shocking. Yet throughout various periods of church history, it was widely accepted.[13]

2. Calvin believed that the Eucharist provides an undoubted assurance of eternal life.

Calvin stated that the sacrament of the Eucharist provided the "undoubted assurance of eternal life to our minds, but also secures the immortality of our flesh."

In context, Calvin is discussing how Christ is present in the sacraments. For Calvin, believers are united with Christ spiritually. It's not that Christ comes down to be physically present in the elements, but that believers, are in a spiritual sense, taken up to heaven during the Lord's Supper to be connected to Jesus spiritually.[14]

3. Calvin believed it was acceptable to lambaste his opponents with vicious names.

Calvin treated his critics with contempt, calling them "'pigs,' asses,' 'riffraff,' 'dogs,' 'idiots,' and 'stinking beasts.'"[15]

In this vein, Calvin said the following words about the great Anabaptist leader Menno Simons:

> Nothing could be prouder, nothing more impudent than this donkey.[16]

4. Calvin believed that some of the Old Testament capital offenses should be enforced today.

The city of Geneva was ruled in part by the clergy. But Calvin's voice was the most influential in the city for a lengthy period of time. One historian put it this way: "From 1541 till his death in 1564 his voice was the most influential in Geneva."[17]

Here are some facts about Geneva while Calvin was in residence there, including capital offenses:[18]

- According to Durant, "The whole household shall attend the sermons on Sunday, except when someone shall be left at home to tend to the children or cattle. If there is preaching on week days, all who can must come—unless there be some good excuse—so that at least one from each household shall be present."[19]
- If a person came to the service after the sermon had begun, he was warned. If he continued to do so, he would have to pay a fine.[20]
- Heresy was regarded as "an insult to God and treason to the state and was punished by death."[21]
- "Witchcraft was a capital crime. In one year, fourteen alleged witches were sent to the stake on the charge that they persuaded Satan to afflict Geneva with the plague."[22]
- Clergy were to abstain from "hunting, gambling, feasting, commerce, secular amusements, and had to accept annual visitations and moral scrutiny by church superiors."[23]

- "Gambling, card-playing . . . frequenting of taverns, dancing . . . indecent or irreligious songs, . . . immodesty in dress" were all prohibited.[24]
- "The allowable color and quantity of clothing, and the number of dishes permissible at a meal, were specified by law."[25]
- "A woman was jailed for arranging her hair in an immodest fashion."[26]
- "Children were to be named not after saints in the Catholic calendar but preferably after Old Testament characters; an obstinate father served four days in prison for insisting on naming his son Claude instead of Abraham."[27]
- "To speak disrespectfully of Calvin or the clergy was a crime. A first violation of these ordinances was punished with a reprimand, further violations with fines, persistent violation with imprisonment or banishment."[28]
- "To laugh at Calvin's sermons, or to have spoken hot words of him in the street, was a crime."[29]
- "Fornication was to be punished with exile or drowning; adultery, blasphemy, or idolatry, with death."[30]
- "In just two years (1558–1559), there were 414 prosecutions for moral offenses."[31]
- "As everywhere in the sixteenth century, torture was often used to obtain confessions or evidence."[32]
- "Calvin's son-in-law and his step-daughter were among those condemned for adultery."[33]
- "The Consistory made little distinction between religion and morality."[34]

- "The extant records of the Council for this period reveal a high percentage of illegitimate children, abandoned infants, forced marriages, and sentences of death."[35]
- "During the seventeen years for which there are reliable records (1542–1564), there were 139 recorded executions in Geneva."[36]

5. Calvin believed that Jewish people were impious, inauthentic, and lacked common sense.

Calvin wrote, "I have had much conversation with many Jews. I have never seen either a drop of piety or a grain of truth or ingenuousness—nay, I have never found common sense in any Jew."[37]

In Calvin's comment on Isaiah 60:6–7, "where the Jews had been promised great 'abundance' and that the 'wealth of the nations shall come unto thee,' Calvin observed: 'Under the pretext of this prophecy, the Jews stupidly devour all the riches of the earth with their unrestrained cupidity.'"[38]

6. Calvin believed that God did not create all humans on equal terms, but created some individuals for eternal damnation.

In popular Calvinism, all humans are born equally in sin, yet out of His mercy, God saves some, leaving the rest in their sin. This idea is known as "double predestination." According to this view, God predestines some to salvation and others to destruction.

While this idea will not be shocking to some Christians, particularly Calvinists, the idea that God would knowingly create some individuals so as to destroy them eternally in the end is shocking to many believers. (Calvinists, on the other hand, are shocked that God chooses to save anyone!) According to Calvin,

> The predestination by which God adopts some to the hope of life, and adjudges others to eternal death, no man who would be thought pious ventures simply to deny. . . . By pre-destination we mean the eternal decree of God, by which he determined with himself whatever he wished to happen with regard to every man. All are not created on equal terms, but some are preordained to eternal life, others to eternal damnation; and, accordingly, as each has been created for one or other of these ends, we say that he has been predestinated to life or to death.[39]

Calvin also stated,

> With Augustine I say: the Lord has created those whom he unquestionably foreknew would go to destruction. This has happened because he has willed.[40]

While this isn't shocking to any Calvinist, to most evangelicals who aren't Reformed, the notion that God wills that anyone would "go to destruction" is a shocking idea. Especially in light of texts like 2 Peter 3:9, "[God is] not willing that any should perish" (NRSV).

Chapter 21 of book 3 of John Calvin's *Institutes of the Christian Religion* is called "Of the Eternal Election, by Which God Has Predestinated Some to Salvation, and Others to Destruction."

Now before any of you become saturated with ill feelings toward Calvin, some historical context will prove helpful.

Calvin lived in an era where theological transgressions were punished by force. Historians have pointed out that Servetus forced Calvin's hand by coming to Geneva. In fact, Calvin pleaded with him to give up his errors. Geneva, like most European cities of that day, was ruled by law, including theological law. Life in Calvin's day was difficult, harsh, and short.

Consequently, brutish communal strictures weren't the exception in Geneva. They were the rule all over. On the flip side, Calvin's Geneva provided pastoral help to the city, even becoming a city of refuge for Protestants who lived all over Europe.

Again, as in all the chapters of this book, the point is *not* to put the greatest influencers of the Christian faith in a bad light or disregard their legacy.

It's the opposite.

It is to show that even the most influential Christians who have changed the lives of countless people for good—Calvin being one of them—believed things that were surprising, shocking, and even outrageous.

So tread carefully the next time you come across another follower of Jesus who doesn't believe just like you do on every doctrinal point. And when you're tempted to verbally slaughter them because of their "bad theology," remember John Calvin—the man whom Charles Spurgeon said had a near flawless theology—and consider some of the other ideas the great Reformer believed.

Let's now look to the man who profoundly shaped both Protestant and Catholic theology.

10

The Shocking Beliefs of Augustine

A spiritually minded man will never come to you with the demand—"Believe this and that"; but with the demand that you square your life with the standards of Jesus. We are not asked to believe the Bible, but to believe the One Whom the Bible reveals (cf. John 5:39–40).

~ Oswald Chambers

Evangelical Christianity owes an enormous debt to Augustine. In fact, there's wide consensus among historians that next to Jesus and Paul, Augustine is the most influential figure in the history of Christianity.

Even *Time* magazine said Augustine is "a major intellectual, spiritual, and cultural force" that continues until this day.[1]

So even though Augustine is considered a Roman Catholic father of the church, many Protestants claim him, including countless evangelicals.

For example, Augustine's influence on both Calvin and Luther (and modern-day evangelicalism as a whole) was remarkable. Even today, many Reformed theologians claim Augustine in their camp. It has been said that the Reformation was essentially a triumph and revival of Augustine's theology.[2]

Augustine was the bishop of Hippo in North Africa in the fourth and fifth centuries. In his undisputed classic, *The City of God*, Augustine answered the prevailing criticism of his day that the Christians were responsible for the fall of Rome.

Augustine wrote more than 1,000 works (all in a day when laptops, desktops, typewriters, and Dragon dictation software didn't exist!).

He's known to have written the very first autobiography in history. His *Confessions* is still considered to be a classic.

Famed historian Will Durant said of Augustine, "He is the most authentic, eloquent, and powerful voice of the Age of Faith in Christendom."[3]

Despite Augustine's titanic intellect, he wrote humbly. He shamelessly admitted that many truths are beyond our understanding. So much so that even additional study of the Scriptures may not resolve them. On this score, he said,

> In matters that are obscure and far beyond our vision, even in such as we may find treated in Holy Scripture, different Interpretations are sometimes possible without prejudice to the faith we have received. In such a case, we should not rush in headlong and so firmly take our stand on one side that, if further progress in the search of truth justly undermines this position, we too fall with it. That would be to battle not for the teaching of Holy Scripture but for our own, wishing its teaching to conform to ours, whereas we ought to wish ours to conform to that of Sacred Scripture.[4]

Much of Augustine's writings are incredibly insightful, forming the basis of the best of modern evangelical theology. However, there are some views of Augustine that many evangelical Christians will find surprising, shocking, or just plain wrong.

Before we launch into our list, here are some of Augustine's more enduring quotes:

> Someone says to me, "Let me understand, in order to believe." I answer, "Believe in order to understand."[5]

> Thou movest us to delight in praising Thee; for thou hast formed us for Thyself, and our hearts are restless till they find rest in Thee.[6]

> Once and for all, I give you this one short command: love, and do what you will.[7]

> The Bible was composed in such a way that as beginners mature, its meaning grows with them.[8]

> What outward appearance, what form, what stature, hands or feet, has love? None can say; and yet love has feet, which take us to the Church, love has hands which give to the poor, love has eyes which give intelligence of him who is in need—as the Psalm says: "Blessed is he who bethinks himself of the needy and poor."[9]

> A portent, therefore, happens not contrary to nature, but contrary to what we know as nature.[10]

> Further, all men are to be loved equally. But since you cannot do good to all, you are to pay special attention to those who, by the accidents of time, or place, or circumstances, are brought into closer connection with you.[11]

For it was my sin, that not in Him, but in His creatures—
myself and others—I sought for pleasures, sublimities,
truths, and so fell headlong into sorrows, confusions,
errors.[12]

To the both of you who believe Roman Catholics should
never be quoted favorably, holster your weapons. Just because
I like these quotes doesn't mean I'm headed toward Rome. I
don't ascribe to Roman Catholic theology, but I have many
friends who are Roman Catholic, and some of them are
among the most godly people on the planet.

That said, here are some of Augustine's beliefs that won't
sit well with many evangelicals.

1. Augustine believed that the purpose of marriage is procreation, and that lust during sex—even among married Christians—was wrong.

In his *Confessions*, Augustine talked openly about his losing
battle with sexual lust during his youth. At age thirty-two, he
became celibate. For Augustine personally, being a Christian
meant abandoning marriage. Significantly, asceticism was
popular during the time in which Augustine lived.[13]

He believed that all sexual intercourse, even within the
bounds of Christian marriage, involved concupiscence (sinful desire or lust).[14]

But for Augustine, celibacy was better.

Undergirding his views on this subject was Augustine's
belief that sex had but one purpose—procreation. Yet he
did believe that married people who enjoyed sex without the
intention of having children could be forgiven.

2. Augustine believed that the use of contraception to prevent children was perverting the purpose of marriage, "committing adultery within marriage" and "turning the bed-chamber into a brothel."

Here's what Augustine said about preventing the birth of children within marriage (that is, the use of contraceptives):

> The doctrine that the production of children is an evil, directly opposes the next precept, "Thou shall not commit adultery;" for those who believe this doctrine, in order that their wives may not conceive, are led to commit adultery even in marriage. They take wives, as the law declares, for the procreation of children; but from this erroneous fear of polluting the substance of the deity, their intercourse with their wives is not of a lawful character; and the production of children, which is the proper end of marriage, they seek to avoid. As the apostle long ago predicted of thee, thou dost indeed forbid to marry, for thou seekest to destroy the purpose of marriage. Thy doctrine turns marriage into an adulterous connection, and the bed-chamber into a brothel.[15]

3. Augustine believed that if you are going to teach Scripture, you must have a knowledge of the natural world, mathematics, music, science, history, the liberal arts, and a mastery of dialectics (the science of disputation).[16]

This standard would rule out most Bible preachers and teachers today. Interestingly, despite his strong emphasis on the need for mastering academic subjects, Augustine could read very little Greek (the original language of the New Testament) and zero Hebrew.

Augustine speaks of an imaginary conversation with Moses, saying, "And should he speak Hebrew, in vain will it strike on my senses, nor would aught of it touch my mind; but if Latin, I should know what he said."[17]

4. Augustine believed that sacramental baptism produces regeneration and is necessary for the forgiveness of sins.

On this point, Augustine's view is echoed by Roman Catholic teaching today. Here are some examples:

> But the sacrament of baptism is undoubtedly the sacrament of regeneration: Wherefore, as the man who has never lived cannot die, and he who has never died cannot rise again, so, he who has never been born cannot be born again.[18]

> Baptism, therefore washes away indeed all sins—absolutely all sins, whether of deed, or words, or thoughts, whether original or added, whether such as are committed in ignorance or allowed in knowledge.[19]

> When ye have been baptized, hold fast to a good life in the commandments of God, that ye may guard your baptism even unto the end. I do not tell you that ye will live here without sin; but they are venial, without which this life is not. For the sake of all sins was Baptism provided; for the sake of light sins, without which we cannot be, was prayer provided. What hath the Prayer? "Forgive us our debts, as we also forgive our debtors." Once for all we have washing in Baptism, every day we have washing in prayer. Only do not commit those things for which ye must needs be separated from Christ's body: which be far from you! For those whom ye have seen doing penance, have committed heinous things,

either adulteries or some enormous crimes: for these they do penance. Because if theirs had been light sins, to blot out these daily prayer would suffice.

In three ways then are sins remitted in the Church; by Baptism, by prayer, by the greater humility of penance; yet God doth not remit sins but to the baptized. The very sins which He remits first, He remits not but to the baptized. When? when they are baptized. The sins which are after remitted upon prayer, upon penance, to whom He remits, it is to the baptized that He remitteth. For how can they say, "Our Father," who are not yet born sons? The Catechumens, so long as they be such, have upon them all their sins. If Catechumens, how much more Pagans? how much more heretics? But to heretics we do not change their baptism. Why? because they have baptism in the same way as a deserter has the soldier's mark: just so these also have Baptism; they have it, but to be condemned thereby, not crowned. And yet if the deserter himself, being amended, begin to do duty as a soldier, does any man dare to change his mark?[20]

5. Augustine believed it was permissible to use force against heretics.

The primary example of Augustine advocating force was against a sect known as the Donatists. The Donatists claimed that certain bishops were ordained by spiritual traitors (those who denied the faith during a period of persecution). Therefore, the Donatists believed traitors didn't deserve to remain church leaders and their ordinations were invalid. The popular leader of this group was Donatus Magnus, after whom they were named.

Augustine bitterly criticized the Donatists and developed his doctrine of the church out of that debate. To Augustine's mind, "the essence of the church is in the union of the whole church with Christ, not in the personal character of certain select Christians."[21]

Augustine advocated the use of force against the Donatists, asking,

> Why, therefore, should not the Church use force in compelling her lost sons to return, if the lost sons compelled others to their destruction? . . . Is it not a part of the care of the shepherd, when any sheep have left the flock, even though not violently forced away, but led astray by tender words and coaxing blandishments, to bring them back to the fold of his master when he has found them, by the fear or even the pain of the whip, if they show symptoms of resistance; especially since, if they multiply with growing abundance among the fugitive slaves and robbers, he has the more right in that the mark of the master is recognized on them, which is not outraged in those whom we receive but do not rebaptize? For the wandering of the sheep is to be corrected in such wise that the mark of the Redeemer should not be destroyed on it.[22]

Part of the reason for this is because the Donatists engaged in violence against other Christians. As a result, Augustine urged the government to exercise its power against them vigorously, retracting his earlier view "that no one should be coerced into the unity of Christ, that we must act only by arguments and prevail by force of reason, lest we should have those whom we knew as avowed heretics feigning themselves to be Catholics."[23]

To Augustine's mind, it was better that a few Donatists suffer than for all to be damned due to a lack of coercion. At the same time, he pleaded consistently that the state officials not enforce the death penalty against heretics.

He wrote,

We do not wish to have the sufferings of the servants of God avenged by the infliction of precisely similar injuries in the way of retaliation. Not, of course, that we object to the removal from these wicked men of the liberty to perpetrate further crimes; but our desire is rather that justice be satisfied without the taking of their lives or the maiming of their bodies in any part, and that, by such coercive measures as may be in accordance with the laws, they be turned from their insane frenzy to the quietness of men in their sound judgment, or compelled to give up mischievous violence and betake themselves to some useful labor. This is indeed called a penal sentence; but who does not see that when a restraint is put upon the boldness of savage violence, and the remedies fitted to produce repentance are not withdrawn, this discipline should be called a benefit rather than vindictive punishment?[24]

6. Augustine believed that the Lord's Supper (the Eucharist) was necessary for salvation.

On this score, he wrote:

The Christians of Carthage have an excellent name for the sacraments, when they say that baptism is nothing else than "salvation," and the sacrament of the body of Christ nothing else than "life." Whence, however, was this derived, but from that primitive, as I suppose, and apostolic tradition, by which the churches of Christ maintain it to be an inherent principle, that without baptism and partaking of the supper of the Lord it is impossible for any man to attain either to the kingdom of God or to salvation and everlasting life?[25]

7. Augustine held to a dualistic view of the world, which was heavily influenced by non-Christian philosophy.

The third-century theologian Tertullian believed that faith and human philosophy had no points of contact. This idea was summed up in his famous question, "What has Athens to do with Jerusalem?"[26]

Augustine was heavily into the classical philosophical tradition of Platonism and Neoplatonism.

In short, his writings synthesized the Bible and Christian theology with classical learning and culture. They shaped both the medieval mind and the teaching curriculum in European universities.

In this connection, some historians have alleged that Augustine blurred the lines between Christianity and paganism, marrying faith and philosophy and creating a world in which paganism *seemed* to disappear. (Some have argued that paganism really didn't disappear; it was merely baptized in Christian garb.)

Even so, Augustine's platonic views reemerged with Thomas Aquinas, who added Aristotle's philosophy to the Christian mix.[27]

Being heavily influenced by the dualistic sect of the Manichaeans (with whom he spent nine years), Augustine continued to embrace a dualistic viewpoint within his theology.

According to Manichaeism, the physical is bad, the spiritual good. The physical, material realm is sinful, the spiritual realm is good. So the two are pitted against one another instead of seen through a Hebraic mindset, which views humanity and the world—the physical and the spiritual—as part of God's good creation.

Augustine's dualism provoked him to leave society and pursue the invisible realities of the spiritual world. (Dualistic thinking is where we get the idea of the secular versus the spiritual.)

Augustine's dualism also influenced some of his theological views, particularly his views on sex—namely, that sexual desire is sinful and sexual lust in procreation transmits that sin.

8. Augustine believed that a person can fall from grace and lose their salvation.

While some evangelicals agree with this idea, others bitterly oppose it. Augustine wrote,

> If, however, being already regenerate and justified, he relapses of his own will into an evil life, assuredly he cannot say, "I have not received," because of his own free choice to evil he has lost the grace of God, that he had received. And if, stung with compunction by rebuke, he wholesomely bewails, and returns to similar good works, or even better, certainly here most manifestly appears the advantage of rebuke. But yet for rebuke by the agency of man to avail, whether it be of love or not, depends only upon God.[28]

> Man, therefore, was thus made upright that, though unable to remain in his uprightness without divine help, he could of his own mere will depart from it.[29]

9. Augustine believed that Mary (mother of Jesus) was a perpetual virgin.

On this subject he wrote,

> A virgin conceives, yet remains a virgin; a virgin is heavy with child; a virgin brings forth her child, yet she is always a virgin.[30]

> Did not holy Virgin Mary both give birth as a virgin and remain a virgin?[31]

> Thus Christ by being born of a virgin, who, before she knew Who was to be born of her, had determined to continue a virgin, chose rather to approve, than to command, holy virginity.[32]

10. Augustine believed in praying for the dead.

Consider his words:

> It is not to be doubted that the dead are aided by prayers of the holy church, and by the salutary sacrifice, and by the alms, which are offered for their spirits; that the Lord may deal with them more mercifully than their sins have deserved. For this, which has been handed down by the Fathers, the universal Church observes.[33]

> There is an ecclesiastical discipline, as the faithful know, when the names of the martyrs are read aloud in that place at the altar of God, where prayer is not offered for them. Prayer, however, is offered for other dead who are remembered. For it is wrong to pray for a martyr, to whose prayers we ought ourselves be commended.[34]

It is then, I say, the same reason which prevents the Church at any time from praying for the wicked angels, which prevents her from praying hereafter for those men who are to be punished in eternal fire; and this also is the reason why, though she prays even for the wicked so long as they live, she yet does not even in this world pray for the unbelieving and godless who are dead. For some of the dead, indeed, the prayer of the Church or of pious individuals is heard; but it is for those who, having been regenerated in Christ, did not spend their life so wickedly that they can be judged unworthy of such compassion, nor so well that they can be considered to have no need of it.[35]

Three More Views to Be Noted

Some scholars and theologians criticize Augustine because he could only read a small amount of Greek and no Hebrew. Nevertheless, he knew the importance of knowing the original biblical languages.

Reading Greek isn't as much of a problem for preachers and teachers today with the wide array of accurate Bible translations and Greek commentaries at our disposal (the same with Hebrew). However, for a fourth-century theologian to influence most of Catholicism and Protestantism, yet lack these skills, presents a big problem in the minds of many.

The reason is that Augustine had to rely on a poor Latin translation of the Bible to do his theology. Consequently, some scholars have called into question several of Augustine's theological interpretations. Namely, these three . . .

(1) Original Sin

There has been a great deal of recent debate over "original sin" in evangelical circles today. It was Augustine who gave the doctrine of original sin a key place in Christian theology.

To Augustine's mind, all humans inherit original sin. Every person sinned in Adam, and therefore, we all share in Adam's crime and subsequent guilt.

Consequently, for Augustine, every infant is subject to eternal death unless baptized.

While some evangelicals hold to this view of original sin, others contest it, believing that although every person is born with a sin nature, their guilt arises from their actual sinful deeds rather than from Adam's sin.

Some scholars believe that Augustine's view is misinformed because he was using a poor translation of the Bible to craft it. The Latin translation he used was excessively literal and ambiguous. Thus, they argue, he misinterpreted Romans 5:12.[36]

In this connection, one of Augustine's fiercest theological sparring partners was Pelagius, the British monk who rejected the idea of original sin. Pelagius believed that the tendency to sin was man's free will choice, not something inherited from Adam. The views of Pelagius were carried on by a bishop named Julian, whom Augustine refuted in his book, *Against Julian*.

And just to add an interesting bit of history, Charles Finney didn't like Augustine's view of original sin (that's putting it mildly). In his own Finney style, here's what he wrote about Augustine's view of natural inability, original sin, and the idea that humans have an inherent sin nature:

This doctrine is a stumbling-block both to the church and the world—infinitely dishonorable to God, and an abomination alike to God and the human intelligence, and should be banished from every pulpit, and from every formula of doctrine, and from the world. It is a relic of heathen philosophy, and was foisted in among the doctrines of Christianity by Augustine, as everyone may know who will take the trouble to examine for himself.[37]

By the way, I wish Charles didn't hold back and told us how he really felt about the matter.

(2) Justification

The second view that's also debated among evangelicals today is Augustine's view of justification. Augustine held to an idea called *infused* righteousness opposed to *imputed* righteousness, which was held by Luther and Calvin. Some writers believe that Augustine "goofed" on this subject and the entire medieval world followed his goof for a thousand years. (John Wesley held that infused righteousness works in tandem with imputed righteousness, while the "New Perspective" scholars set the debate in a context outside of the imputed versus infused framework.)

Since my intention isn't to provoke a doctrinal shoot-out that gets bogged down in the wheels of arcane theological minutiae, I'll just leave the point there and you can pursue it further on your own if it interests you.

(3) Hell

The third view that some evangelicals today reject—while others strongly believe it—is Augustine's idea that hell was conscious and eternal torment. Augustine claimed that since the salamander can live in fire, it follows that God can make physical bodies that are susceptible to the pain of fire and yet not be damaged by it.[38]

Augustine also believed that hell was under the earth and that the suffering of hell is compounded because God continues to love the people in hell who are not able to return that love.[39]

Incidentally, please don't ask me for an analysis on the anatomy of hell. I've never been there and don't intend to go—thanks to the Lord Jesus Christ. But whatever you surmise it to be, the Scriptures are clear that it's not a place in which you'll ever want to land.

All told, Augustine made a positive mark on the Christian church. Yet he held to a number of strange, if not flawed, viewpoints about God and the teachings of Scripture. Let us, therefore, regrace.

We'll now turn our attention to the founder of an entire tribe of Christians who are still with us today.

11

The Shocking Beliefs of John Wesley

I have never met the man I could despair of after discerning what lies in me apart from the grace of God.

~ Oswald Chambers

John Wesley was remarkable. In his effort to preach the gospel, he is estimated to have traveled between 225,000 and
250,000 miles mainly on horseback. He preached over 40,000
sermons. Standing at only five feet three and weighing between 125 and 128 pounds, Wesley left an indelible mark on
church history.[1]

Perhaps his most enduring contribution is that he gave us
experiential salvation—a salvation experience that moved
past the frontal lobe.

As is the case with all who have the hand of God on them,
Wesley faced unbelievable opposition from every quarter. He

amassed a boatload of enemies. Even members of his own family caused him grief in his ministry.[2]

Yet despite the continuous onslaught against his ministry, God's protection was on him. Wesley's legacy has impacted hundreds of thousands of Christians in every generation, including our own.

Wesley habitually read the New Testament in Greek. One of his most enduring legacies in the realm of Bible interpretation was his work on 1 John. (Yes, 1 John—that's the book that Christians read under their beds with a flashlight and lose their salvation after they've finished!)

For Wesley, 1 John was the capstone of biblical revelation and the synthesis of all he had written.

That said, I'm aware that many Reformed Christians, both in the past and today, regard Wesley as a dangerous heretic. But to my Reformed friends, consider what the following respected Reformed leaders had to say about him:

> I can only say concerning him that, while I detest many of the doctrines which he preached, yet for the man himself I have a reverence second to no Wesleyan; and if there were wanted two apostles to be added to the number of the twelve, I do not believe that there could be found two men more fit to be so added than George Whitefield and John Wesley.[3]
>
> ~ Charles Spurgeon

> Then let us thank God for what John Wesley *was*, and not keep pouring over his deficiencies, and only talking of what he *was not*. Whether we like it or not, John Wesley was a mighty instrument in God's hand for good; and, next to

George Whitefield, was the first and foremost evangelist of England a hundred years ago.

~ J. C. Ryle[4]

I honour and esteem you; I pray for your success and sincerely rejoin in it. I know no one to whom my heart is more united in affection, nor to whom I owe more, as an instrument of Divine grace.

~ John Newton[5]

Interestingly, Wesley's teaching on "heart religion" was almost identical to Jonathan Edwards's teaching on the "religious affections." Nevertheless, Wesley—like every other servant of God—had feet of clay. And he also held to some strange beliefs.

Here are some of them.

1. Wesley believed that church buildings should separate men and women.

Wesley believed that religious buildings should "be parted in the middle by a rail running all along, to divide the men from the women."[6]

2. Wesley believed in ghosts and other paranormal phenomena.

Wesley believed there was a ghost known as "Old Jeffrey" in the Epworth parsonage where he grew up. Wesley actually believed the "ghost" was a demon or a messenger of Satan, sent to afflict his father for his rash promise of leaving the family.[7]

3. Like Augustine before him, Wesley believed in the perpetual virginity of Mary, Jesus' earthly mother.

The difference, of course, is that Augustine was Catholic while Wesley was not. In his "Letter to a Roman Catholic," Wesley stated,

> I believe that he [Jesus] was made man, joining the human nature with the divine in one person; being conceived by the singular operation of the Holy Ghost, and born of the blessed Virgin Mary, who, as well after as before she brought him forth, continued a pure and unspotted virgin.[8]

4. Wesley had a static electricity machine and thought it was a good idea for people to be "electrified daily" for their health.

Wesley lived in the age of Ben Franklin and was fascinated by Franklin, consuming his work on electricity. Interestingly, a replica of Wesley's electricity machine can still be viewed in his London home.[9]

5. According to his *Primitive Physick*, some of Wesley's prescriptions for medical ailments are strange at best.

For sinus colds, Wesley recommended curling up an orange peel and inserting it into one's nostrils. (Don't try that at home!) Wesley's exact words were, "A Cold in the Head. Pare a very thin rind of an orange, roll it up inside out, and thrust a roll into each nostril."[10]

For breast cancer, Wesley recommended applying red poppy water, plantain and rose water mixed with honey and roses. He also said that taking a cold bath regularly was a known cure.[11]

Note that Wesley cared deeply for the sick and was a bit of an experimentalist in that regard.[12]

6. In his library, Wesley owned the "subversive literature" of Miguel de Molinos, Madame Guyon, François Fénelon, and other Christian mystics.

Although he disagreed with the mystics' tendency to draw away from the world, Wesley believed in a mystical quest for God.[13]

This belief made him persona non grata with those Christians who held to a more conservative, objective view of the spiritual life.

7. Wesley believed that wearing jewelry and costly clothes was sinful and that Christians weren't to engage in such behavior.

Specifically, Wesley was strongly against both women and men wearing rings, earrings, and necklaces.[14]

Consequently, the early Methodists were known for their plain dress and absence of jewelry. The Methodist Church upheld Wesley's stance on apparel and jewelry until 1852. In 1852, Wesley's dress code changed because the Methodist manual "no longer regulated the dress and jewelry of the clergy or the people."[15]

8. Wesley was a big fan of the controversial early church figure Montanus.

Wesley regarded Montanus as being "one of the best men then upon earth," who "under the character of a prophet" had revived "what was decayed, and reforming what might be amiss."[16]

Wesley said,

> It seems, therefore, by the best information we can procure at this distance of time, that Montanus was not only a truly good man, but one of the best men then upon earth; and that his real crime was, the severely reproving those who professed themselves Christians, while they neither had the mind that was in Christ, nor walked as Christ walked; but were conformable both in their temper and practice to the present evil world.[17]

Montanus, however, is regarded by many evangelicals as a "dangerous heretic." You can research this yourself.

In our next chapter, we'll explore the surprising views of the man who many regard to be the greatest preacher in history.

12

The Shocking Beliefs
of Charles Spurgeon

Beware of being obsessed with consistency to your
own convictions instead of being devoted to God. . . .
It is easier to be an excessive fanatic than it is to be
consistently faithful, because God causes an amazing
humbling of our religious conceit when we are faithful to Him.

~ Oswald Chambers

Charles Haddon Spurgeon is regarded by many to be the
greatest preacher in history. According to one historical
source, "there is available more material written by Spurgeon
than any other Christian author, living or dead."[1]

Spurgeon's collection of sermons contains over twenty
million words. He is alleged to have read approximately six
books a week and seemingly had a photographic memory.

His voice was so powerful that he once preached to an audience of over 23,000 people without the aid of a microphone.[2]

For these reasons, Spurgeon is often called "the prince of preachers" and "the preacher's preacher."

During his day, Spurgeon was the pastor of the largest Protestant church in the world. He ran an orphanage, provided oversight to sixty-seven charity organizations, and directed a theological school. He also authored approximately 150 books.

A missionary in Africa is purported to have once asked Spurgeon, "How do you manage to do two men's work in a single day?" Spurgeon's response was, "You have forgotten there are two of us . . . and the one you see the least of, often does the most work."[3]

To his credit, Spurgeon also spoke out strongly against slavery. So much so that American publishers began deleting his anti-slavery remarks from their publications.[4]

Yet despite the impressive ministry that Spurgeon had, he held to some strange—and even shocking—beliefs. Here are some of them.

1. Spurgeon was never ordained and didn't believe that ordination was important. He was also against the use of honorific titles.

This one has been alarming to many Reformed people, which is Spurgeon's own tribe, who hold ordination as well as honorific titles such as "Reverend" in high regard.

Here's an excerpt taken from a lengthy diatribe from Spurgeon on these subjects:

Whence comes the whole paraphernalia of ordination as observed among some Dissenters? Since there is no special gift to bestow, why in any case the laying on of empty hands? . . . A man who has preached for years is Mr. Brown, but after his ordination or recognition he develops into the Reverend Mr. Brown; what important change has he undergone? . . . Here are reverend students of an unreverend preacher, the title being given to the one out of courtesy, and withheld from the other for the same reason. . . . We do not object to a recognition of the choice of the church by its neighbors and their ministers, on the contrary, we believe it to be a fraternal act, sanctioned by the very spirit of Christianity; but where it is supposed to be essential, is regarded as a ceremony, and is thought to be the crowning feature of the settlement, we demur.

He goes on to denounce the idea that spiritual duties can only be carried out by the ordained.

[There is] the notion in some churches *that only an ordained or recognized minister should preside at the Lord's table.* Small is our patience with this unmitigated Popery, and yet it is by no means uncommon. Pulpits which are most efficiently supplied on other Sundays by men who are without pastoral charge must be vacated by them on the first Sunday of the month because the friends like a stated minister to *administer the sacrament.*

. . . *The benediction is in some regions almost as sacredly reserved for the minister as the absolution for the priest* in Popish churches. We heard it remarked the other day as quite a singular thing that a non-ministerial brother, being in the chair at a religious meeting, had actually pronounced the benediction. . . . Here was a mere layman thinking himself as able to invoke a blessing upon the assembly as the clerics around him! The brethren around us expressed their pleasure that he had done so, but even this showed that it was rather an innovation, very commendable, no doubt, in these days, but still an innovation.

And still more,

It seems rather odd to us that a man should print upon his visiting card the fact that he is a reverend person. Why does he not occasionally vary the term, and call himself estimable, amiable, talented, or beloved? Would this seem odd? Is there any valid objection to such a use of adjectives after the fashion is once set by employing the word *reverend*? . . . Why do we not, like members of secret orders and others, go in for Worthy Masterships and Past Grands, and the like? . . . It may be said that the title of reverend is only one of courtesy, but then so was the title of Rabbi among the Jews, yet the disciples were not to be called Rabbi.[5]

2. Spurgeon believed smoking cigars was not wrong, and it could be done "to the glory of God."

Spurgeon was a frequent cigar smoker, and this provoked condemnation from many of his fellow Christians who believed that using tobacco—in any form—was a sin.

Here's an excerpt from a lengthy letter that Spurgeon wrote to the *Daily Telegraph* on September 23, 1874, responding to his critics about cigar smoking:

I demur altogether and most positively to the statement that to smoke tobacco is in itself a sin. It may become so, as any other indifferent action may, but as an action it is no sin.

Together with hundreds of thousands of my follow-Christians I have smoked, and, with them, I am under the condemnation of living in habitual sin, if certain accusers are to be believed. As I would not knowingly live even in the smallest violation of the law of God, and sin in the transgression of the law, I will not own to sin when I am not conscious of it.

There is growing up in society a Pharisaic system which adds to the commands of God the precepts of men; to that system I will not yield for an hour. The preservation of my liberty may bring upon me the upbraidings of many good men, and the sneers of the self-righteous; but I shall endure both with serenity so long as I feel clear in my conscience before God.

The expression "smoking to the glory of God" standing alone has an ill sound, and I do not justify it; but in the sense in which I employed it I still stand to it. No Christian should do anything in which he cannot glorify God; and this may be done, according to Scripture, in eating and drinking and the common actions of life.

When I have found intense pain relieved, a weary brain soothed, and calm, refreshing sleep obtained by a cigar, I have felt grateful to God, and have blessed His name; this is what I meant, and by no means did I use sacred words triflingly.[6]

Spurgeon is reported to have also said this on the subject:

Why, a man may think it a sin to have his boots blacked. Well, then, let him give it up, and have them whitewashed. I wish to say that I'm not ashamed of anything whatever that I do, and I don't feel that smoking makes me ashamed, and therefore I mean to smoke to the glory of God.[7]

3. Spurgeon believed going into debt was not acceptable.

He felt so strongly about this that he was willing to sell his means of transportation (which was necessary for him to travel and minister) to avoid debt.

> I paid as large sums as I could from my own income, and resolved to spend all I had, and then take the cessation of my means as a voice from the Lord to stay the effort, as I am firmly persuaded that we ought under no pretense to go into debt. On one occasion I proposed the sale of my horse and carriage, although these were almost absolute necessities to me on account of continual journeys in preaching the Word.[8]

Spurgeon felt everyone should spend well below their means and the first thing they should cut out was beer money. Here's a quote:

> If our poor people could only see the amount of money which they melt away in drink, their hair would stand on end with fright. Why, they swallow rivers of beer, seas of porter, and great big lakes of spirits and other fire waters. We should all be clothed like gentlemen and live like fighting cocks if what is wasted on booze could be sensibly used. We would need to get up earlier in the morning to spend all our money, for we would find ourselves suddenly made quite rich, and all that through stopping the drip of the tap. . . . If young men would deny themselves, work hard, live hard, and save in their early days, they need not keep their noses to the grindstone all their lives, as many have to do. Let them be teetotalers for economy's sake; water is the strongest drink, it drives mills. It's the drink of lions and horses, and Samson never drank anything else. The beer money would soon build a house.[9]

4. Spurgeon thought the idle (those who didn't work) were beyond hope and it wasn't worth wasting time trying to improve them.

Spurgeon was a workaholic and put immense pressure on others to work hard, just as he did.

On this score, he said,

> Lazy lie-a-beds are not working men at all, any more than pigs are bullocks or thistles apple trees. All are not hunters that wear red coats, and all are not working men who call themselves so. I wonder sometimes that some of our employers keep so many cats who catch no mice. I would as soon drop my halfpence down a well as pay some people for pretending to work. It only irritates you and makes your flesh crawl to see them all day creeping over a cabbage leaf. Live and let live, say I, but I don't include sluggards in that license. "They who will not work, neither let them eat."[10]

According to one of Spurgeon's biographers,

> His [Spurgeon's] first words of rebuke are for the idle, for whom he, as a busy man, seems to have had a great antipathy. . . . He saw no use for idlers except to make the grass grow in the churchyard when they die.[11]

5. Spurgeon did not believe in allowing music in worship.

Spurgeon "tolerated an American organ in mission services," but otherwise, he allowed no instruments at all except on very rare occasions. In general, "Spurgeon had a rooted objection to instrumental music in the worship of God."[12]

6. Spurgeon leaned left in his politics.

Spurgeon experts have pointed out that he was essentially a "left-winger" politically. Spurgeon typically aligned himself with the political views of Prime Minister William Gladstone (who was liberal) instead of the more conservative Benjamin Disraeli, especially when it came to military expansion.

Spurgeon was an advocate of civil rights for people considered "minorities." In the 1800 election, he is said to have single-handedly swung the election in favor of the Liberals against the Conservative Party.[13]

From his own lips, Spurgeon said, "I am as good a Liberal as any man living, and my loving admiration of Mr. Gladstone is the same as ever, hearty and deep."[14]

That said, Spurgeon was also strongly pro-life, railing against the wickedness of abortion which he believed was infanticide. He also believed that God blesses nations who honor Him. So while Spurgeon was often liberal in his politics, he was conservative on some social issues.[15]

7. Spurgeon believed that the supernatural healing of sicknesses still occurred.

While this won't be shocking to contemporary Charismatics and Pentecostals, many of his own tribe (Baptists and Reformed) would find it shocking.

Knowing the latter, Spurgeon hesitated to champion divine healing publicly. Because he didn't want people to view him as a faith healer, he would often pray for the sick incognito, in sickrooms and private studies.[16]

He kept his remarkable encounters with healing close to his vest, again, probably to keep people from lumping him in with faith healers.[17]

8. Spurgeon believed that even the strongest of Christians may face seasons of depression, despair, and doubt.

This may come as a surprise to those who believe that the Christian life should always be full of victory, faith, and joy.

Spurgeon struggled with depression often. He allegedly owned over thirty books on mental health, and he called his depression "a prophet in rough clothing."

Note his words:

> This depression comes over me whenever the Lord is preparing a larger blessing for my ministry; the cloud is black before it breaks, and overshadows before it yields its deluge of mercy. Depression has now become to me as a prophet in rough clothing, a John the Baptist, heralding the nearer coming of my Lord's richer benison.[18]

9. Spurgeon believed he heard God's voice, and it told him to keep preaching without a college education.

While this won't surprise many Charismatics or Pentecostals, the fact is, Spurgeon was Reformed. While not all Reformed people deny the present-day function of miraculous gifts, many do. Scholars debate whether the voice that Spurgeon heard was audible or merely an impression. Spurgeon himself said the voice "may have been a singular illusion."

Referring to Spurgeon's decision to continue preaching without a college education, one biographer writes,

> But it is certain that Mr. Spurgeon evidently believed it was the voice of God. At all events, he allowed it to guide him to the most important decision of his life and ever after kept the saying of that voice vividly before his mind to determine his actions in situations of great difficulty.[19]

In Spurgeon's words:

> That afternoon having to preach at a village station, I walked slowly in a meditating frame of mind, over Midsummer Common, to the little wooden bridge which leads to Chesterton, and in the midst of the Common I was startled by what seemed to me to be a loud voice, but which may have been a singular illusion; whatever it was, the impression it made on my mind was most vivid; I seemed very distinctly to hear the words, "Seekest thou great things for thyself, seek them not!" This led me to look at my position from a different point of view, and to challenge my motives and intentions.[20]

10. Spurgeon believed in what some would call giving "prophetic words" to people, knowing things about them beyond natural means.

Spurgeon not only believed in the current operation of the prophetic gift, he even exercised it, calling out the sins of people he didn't know. Here is an example:

> At the Monday evening prayer-meeting . . . [Spurgeon] mentioned the sermon at Exeter Hall, in which he suddenly broke off from his subject, and, pointing in a certain direction,

said, "Young man, those gloves you are wearing have not been paid for; you have stolen them from your employer." At the close of the service, a young man, looking very pale and greatly agitated, came to the room which was used as a vestry, and begged for a private interview with Mr. Spurgeon. On being admitted, he placed a pair of gloves upon the table, and tearfully said, "It's the first time I have robbed my master, and I will never do it again. You won't expose me, sir, will you? It would kill my mother if she heard that I had become a thief."[21]

The result was the young man's conversion.

In another example, Spurgeon made this remark, exhibiting a supernatural "word of knowledge": "There's a man in the gallery with a bottle of gin in his pocket."[22]

11. Spurgeon believed God answered the prayers of people before they were converted to Christ.

Speaking of himself, Spurgeon said, "God had answered my prayers while I was a child, and before I was converted."

This belief was radical in a society that believed God only heard the prayers of Christians. And some of Spurgeon's hyper-Calvinist detractors found fault with it.

There's no question that Spurgeon is one of the greats in church history. However, seeing that much of what he believed would raise the eyebrows of many believers today, how about extending more grace to those fellow Christians with whom you disagree?

Let's now look at the individual who many believe to be the father of modern evangelism.

13

The Shocking Beliefs of D. L. Moody

God never gives us discernment in order that we may
criticize, but that we may intercede.

~ Oswald Chambers

D. L. Moody is one of my favorite movers and shakers in
church history.

He—along with A. W. Tozer, Charles Spurgeon, G. Campbell Morgan—was a powerful witness to God's sod-turning
tendency for mightily using people who didn't possess a for-
mal theological education, much like the first followers of
Jesus Himself (Paul of Tarsus being the exception).

In Moody's case, he was poorly educated across the board,
yet the hand of God was undeniably on his life. According to
one historian, "The first time he applied for church membership, it was denied him because he failed an oral examination
on Christian doctrine."[1]

In fact, an eighteen-year-old Moody couldn't give a satisfactory answer to a basic Sunday school question.

Moody was asked, "What has Christ done for you, and for us all, that especially entitles Him to our love and obedience?" Moody's response was, "I think He has done a great deal for us all, but I don't know of anything He has done in particular."

Because of that answer, there was not "satisfactory evidence of conversion." Moody was subsequently mentored and was received into membership at his second examination.

Moody's answer was probably due to his being raised in the Unitarian Church, and it was only at seventeen years old that he was exposed to the gospel.[2]

So if we can be patient with a young Moody (especially seeing how he turned out), let's be patient with each other, eh?

Moody served the soldiers in the Civil War, and President Lincoln visited his famous Sunday school. In addition, President Grant attended a revival meeting led by Moody.

It's speculated that he reached 100 million people through his speaking (and writing) in a day when televangelists, radio preachers, podcasts, blogs, and Al Gore (*ahem*, the internet) didn't exist.[3]

Have you ever heard the statement, "God hates sin, but loves the sinner"? Moody helped popularize that statement.

Here are three other "Moodyisms":

Character is what a man is in the dark.[4]

If there had been a committee appointed, Noah's ark would never have been built.[5]

And my favorite one of all,

> You know that some men grow smaller and smaller on an intimate acquaintance; but my experience is that the more and more you know of Christ, the larger He becomes.[6]

Armed with a fifth-grade education, noted as a horrible speller with a poor vocabulary, and void of any theological training, Moody managed to found several schools. The Bible college and publishing house that carry his name still exist. This is quite surprising given how poorly educated he was.[7]

Moody was essentially a "lay evangelist." He wasn't an ordained minister nor a trained theologian or scholar. In fact, firsthand observers got the impression that he was little more than a country bumpkin. Yet he was incredibly effective in reaching people with the gospel of Christ.[8]

Another thing that impresses me about Moody was his heart for the poor. When he began his ministry in the Chicago slums (called "Little Hell" because of its danger), Moody was barely into his twenties. He had a heart for the least, the last, and the lost, spending all of his savings to help the indigent, even risking harm to himself.[9]

All told, here are some beliefs that Moody held that were shocking during his time, some of which may unsettle some evangelicals today.

1. Moody seldom preached on hell.

This was shocking in a day when eighteenth- and nineteenth-century revivalists and evangelists made "hell" a major point in their preaching.

When Moody caught criticism for this, his response was, "A great many people say I don't preach on the terrors of religion. I don't want to—don't want to scare men into the kingdom of God."[10]

Because the love of God broke his own heart, Moody opted to preach God's love and avoid the subject of hell in most of his sermons.[11]

2. Moody espoused the idea of premillennialism (that Jesus would return before the millennium).

While this view isn't shocking to fans of the Left Behind films and books, Moody "was the first premillennial evangelist of note in North American history (the rest were postmillennialists)."[12]

He was also important to the entire history of the development of dispensationalism and the eventual rise and dominance of premillennialism.

That said, Moody was not precise about the details of Christ's second coming, so we cannot be sure of his exact views on the subject. In a sermon entitled "When My Lord Jesus Comes," Moody said, "You should study the Bible for yourself, and come to your own conclusion."[13]

So for those who believe that certainty about last things (eschatology) is a requirement for ministry, Moody's lack of certainty to the timing of the rapture and his lack of dogmatism on end times in general would alarm some Christians today.

3. Moody embraced the Christian evolutionist Henry Drummond as being the most Christlike man he ever met.

Such an "endorsement" was shocking in Moody's day. And it will certainly raise the ire of Christians who damn other believers with the guilt-by-association card.

Moody was viciously attacked as a "heretic" simply because he allowed Drummond to speak at some of his Christian conferences. There's good reason to believe that he lost sizable financial support as a result.

Drummond was written off by many Christians because he believed that God created humans through the mechanism of evolution. Drummond wrote the book *The Ascent of Man*, published in 1894. The book attempted to harmonize Christianity and evolution, as a number of people tried to do in the early stages of the popularity of evolutionary theory. Even one of my Reformed heroes, B. B. Warfield, dabbled with the legitimacy of evolution.

Moody rejected evolutionary theory, but that didn't dissuade him from befriending and endorsing Henry Drummond. Nor did it dissuade others from condemning Moody with the same vitriol that they leveled against Drummond. (Regrettably, this sort of thing still happens today in the Christian world.)[14]

4. Moody didn't exclude women from ministry and even allowed them to preach to the congregation.

Again, a shocker for his time. And in the minds of contemporary Christians who believe women should be muzzled (I mean excluded) from ministering to men, what Moody believed about this is considered "unbiblical."[15]

5. Moody didn't believe in making doctrine an issue.

For this reason, some Calvinists and Arminians claimed him on the one hand, but they were infuriated by him on the other.

The Arminians broke out in hives over his "once in grace, always in grace" view. And Calvinists were livid over his emphasis on human responsibility, faith-is-a-choice view, and his belief in the universal provision of salvation.

According to Moody, "I don't try to reconcile God's sovereignty and man's free agency."[16]

That statement didn't endear him to either Calvinists or Arminians.

6. Moody believed in interdenominational ecumenicism.

This also disturbed hard-core Calvinists and Arminians.

Moody embraced the liberal causes of social reform, church unity, and ecumenicism, but he also embraced the conservative causes of premillennialism in his evangelistic efforts (believing that the world was a sinking ship, and Christians were obligated to rescue as many as possible before the ship sank).

Moody was seen as a bridge between conservatives and liberals, combining issues that polarized both sides. This quote by Moody captures his heart on the matter:

> Talk not of this sect and that sect, this party and that party; but solely and exclusively of the great, comprehensive cause of Jesus Christ . . . there should be one faith, one mind, one spirit. . . . Let us . . . contend for Christ only. . . . Oh that God may so fill us with his love and the love of souls, that no

thought of minor sectarian parties can come in; that there may be no room for them in our atmosphere whatever; and that the Spirit of God may give us one mind and one spirit here to glorify His holy name.[17]

Over the course of his ministry, Moody learned, however, that transcending the hard-core left and the hard-core right is a dangerous place in which to live, because both sides take dead aim at you!

7. Moody found some of the Roman Catholic mystics to be helpful.

This one would have gotten him tarred and feathered by a number of Christian groups today. In his *One Thousand and One Thoughts from My Library*, Moody cites 225 authors; included are the Christian mystics, Madame Guyon and Madame Swetchine. (Guyon's writings have been frowned on by many in the Roman Church, so much so that at one point they were placed on the list of prohibited books index!)[18]

Regarding Moody's views on Catholic teaching, "he preached against transubstantiation . . . and the confessional and priestly absolution," but he also "advocated co-operation with Roman Catholics in world evangelization" and "'gave a handsome sum' to build a Roman Catholic church in his home town." In addition, Moody once asked a "Roman Catholic bishop to pray for him."[19]

8. Moody believed all Ten Commandments were binding on Christians, with penalties for violators, and he criticized preachers for not emphasizing them enough.

What makes this surprising is that Moody criticized his mentor Charles Spurgeon on these very grounds saying,

> I do not remember ever to have heard a sermon preached on the commandments. I have an index of two thousand five hundred sermons preached by Spurgeon, and not one of them selects its text from the first seventeen verses of Exodus 20. The people must be made to understand that the Ten Commandments are still binding, and that there is a penalty attached to their violation. We do not want a gospel of mere sentiment. The Sermon on the Mount did not blot out the Ten Commandments.[20]

Many Christians today are divided over the role of the Law of Moses in the life of the Christian. Some believe the Sabbath command was fulfilled in Christ, contending that Christians aren't obligated to keep Saturday (which some say is the true Sabbath) holy.[21]

On the other hand, Moody believed that a countless number of "careless Christians" will get to heaven by "the skin of their teeth." On this score, he wrote,

> Moreover, it seems highly probable, indeed I think it is clearly taught by Scripture, that a great many careless Christians will get into heaven. There will be a great many who will get in "by the skin of their teeth," or as Lot was saved from Sodom, "so as by fire." They will barely get in, but there will be no crown of rejoicing. But *everybody* is not going to rush into heaven. There are a great many who will *not* be there.[22]

I come back to the front of this chapter. Moody was an evangelical superstar, and for good reason. That being said, he wasn't flawless in his views. Let's, therefore, regrace, shall we?

In our next chapter, we'll examine the surprising beliefs of the best-known Christian leader of the twentieth century.

14

Seven Shocking Statements by Billy Graham

True intercession involves bringing the person, or the circumstance that seems to be crashing in on you, before God, until you are changed by His attitude toward that person or circumstance.

~ Oswald Chambers

Billy Graham is an icon.

Few people in history have impacted the Christian faith like Graham. While he has his critics—like every other servant of God—countless positive things can be said about him, all remarkable. Throughout his lifetime, Graham preached to an estimated 215 million people in more than 417 crusades.

In the summer of 2005, during his final evangelistic crusade, he preached to a quarter of a million people over a three-day span.

In addition to his remarkable preaching ministry, Graham prayed with or counseled twelve American presidents.[1]

In my humble (but accurate) opinion, Graham was one of the "greats."

That said, here are seven little-known shocking quotes from Billy Graham. Graham isn't noted for being an "out-of-the-box" nontraditionalist, but these quotes show a side of him that runs against traditional evangelical thinking.

Whether you agree with the sentiment of these quotes or not, they will surprise many evangelicals.

Quote 1—Are Muslims and Buddhists Saved? (an Interview with Robert Schuller)

Schuller: Tell me, what do you think is the future of Christianity?

Graham: Well, Christianity and being a true believer, you know, I think there's the body of Christ, which comes from all the Christian groups around the world, or outside the Christian groups. I think everybody that loves Christ, or knows Christ, whether they're conscious of it or not, they're members of the body of Christ. And I don't think that we're going to see a great sweeping revival that will turn the whole world to Christ at any time. I think James answered that, the apostle James in the first council in Jerusalem, when he said that God's purpose for this age is to call out a people for His name. And that's what God is doing today, He's calling people out of the world for His name, whether they come from the Muslim world, or the Buddhist world, or the Christian world or the nonbelieving world, they are members of the body of Christ because they've been called by God. They may not even know the name of Jesus but they know in their hearts that they need something that they don't have, and they turn to the only light that they have, and I think that they are saved, and that they're going to be with us in heaven.

Schuller: What I hear you saying is that it's possible for Jesus Christ to come into human hearts and soul and life even if they've been born in darkness and never had an exposure to the Bible. Is that a correct interpretation of what you are saying?

Graham: Yes, it is because I believe that. I've met people in various parts of the world in tribal situations, that they have never seen a Bible or heard about a Bible, and never heard of Jesus, but they've believed in their hearts that there was a God, and they've tried to live a life that was quite apart from the surrounding community in which they lived.

Schuller: That's fantastic, I'm so thrilled to hear you say that, there's a wideness in God's mercy.

Graham: There is. There definitely is.[2]

Quote 2—Salvation without Christ? (an Interview with *McCall's* Magazine)

I used to play God, but I can't do that anymore. I used to believe pagans in far-off countries were lost—were going to hell—if they did not have the Gospel of Jesus Christ preached to them. I no longer believe that. . . . I believe there are other ways of recognizing the existence of God—through nature, for instance—and plenty of other opportunities, therefore, of saying "yes" to God. (Graham later clarified what he meant here.)[3]

Quote 3—Should We Link America with the Kingdom of God?

Speaking as an American himself, Graham said:

> I came close to identifying the American way of life with the kingdom of God. Then I realized that God had called me to a higher kingdom than America. I have tried to be faithful to my calling as a minister of the gospel.[4]

Quote 4—Staying Out of Politics

Looking back on his long history of speaking and traveling, Billy Graham made this comment:

> I wouldn't have taken so many speaking engagements, including some of the things I did over the years that I probably didn't really need to do—weddings and funerals and building dedications, things like that. . . . I also would have steered clear of politics. I'm grateful for the opportunities God gave me to minister to people in high places; people in power have spiritual and personal needs like everyone else, and often they have no one to talk to. But looking back I know I sometimes crossed the line, and I wouldn't do that now.[5]

Quote 5—More Worship, Less Works

In response to an interviewer who asked Graham this question, "If you were to do things over again, would you do it differently?" he said,

> Yes. I would study more. I would pray more. Travel less. Take less speaking engagements. I took too many of them, in too many places around the world. If I had to do it over

again, I would spend more time in meditation and prayer, and just telling the Lord how much I love Him and adore Him, and I'm looking forward to the time we're going to spend together for eternity.[6]

This response may be surprising to those who believe that the name of the game in Christianity is service. Graham later realized that it's not.

Quote 6—Has the Church Denied the Authoritative Biblical Message?

Here is Billy Graham's prediction about the future Christian landscape. He made it in 1965, and it has since come to pass.

Because the church, in turning to naturalistic religion, increasingly proclaims a humanistic gospel, thousands of laymen and clergymen alike are asking penetrating questions about the purpose and mission of the church. Thousands of loyal church members, particularly in America, are beginning to meet in prayer groups and Bible study classes. Multitudes of Christians within the church are moving toward the point where they may reject the institution that we call the church. They are beginning to turn to more simplified forms of worship. They are hungry for a personal and vital experience with Jesus Christ. They want a heartwarming personal faith.

Unless the church quickly recovers its authoritative biblical message, we may witness the spectacle of millions of Christians going outside the institutional church to find spiritual food.[7]

Quote 7—A Successful Minister Does Not Spend Most of His Time with a Great Crowd

In the following quote, Graham answers the question "If you were a pastor of a large church in a principal city, what would be your plan of action?":

> I think one of the first things I would do would be to get a small group of eight or ten or twelve men around me that would meet a few hours a week and pay the price! It would cost them something in time and effort. I would share with them everything I have, over a period of years. Then I would actually have twelve ministers among the laymen who in turn could take eight or ten or twelve more and teach them. I know one or two churches that are doing that, and it is revolutionizing the church. Christ, I think, set the pattern. He spent most of his time with twelve men. He didn't spend it with great crowds. In fact, every time he had a great crowd it seems to me that there weren't too many results. The great results, it seems to me, came in his personal interview and in the time he spent with the twelve.[8]

Graham is certainly one of the greats who shaped the Christian church, but even he had some surprising views. I don't think I have to repeat the lesson at this point.

15

The New Tolerance

The only way to keep true to God is by a steady persistent refusal to be interested in Christian work and to be interested alone in Jesus Christ.

~ Oswald Chambers

If you are alive, you've noticed. But perhaps this chapter will provide language for it.

We live in a day where there is profound intolerance exercised in the name of tolerance. I call it "the new tolerance."

It goes something like this:

"If you don't agree with *my* beliefs and *my* value system, then you're intolerant."

Which being interpreted means "In the name of tolerance, I'm intolerant of everyone who doesn't bow to my values and beliefs."

Or . . .

"I'm intolerant of everyone except those who agree with me, and in the name of tolerance, I will brand them intolerant."

What is tolerance?

True tolerance doesn't force people to adopt a belief system, whatever it may be.

True tolerance can "agree to disagree" and go on with one's life in peace without ever entering into a social media beatdown over politics, ethics, or theology.

True tolerance values all mortals as made in God's image, and therefore, regards them worthy of love. At the same time, it points out areas of disagreement and even condemns beliefs and actions that violate God's will.

Disagreeing with a person's habits, values, or ideas isn't the equivalent of hating, fearing, despising, or wishing them ill.

Loving a person doesn't mean approving their practices or beliefs.

Love and approval aren't the same thing.

Even God doesn't always approve those whom He loves.

Jesus, who is the human face of God, said as much:

He is kind to the ungrateful and wicked. (Luke 6:35)

By contrast, the new tolerance says, "I will tolerate everything except those who disagree with me."

That, dear friends, is an extremely intolerant tolerance.

Let it not be so among the people of God.

16

You Just Might Be a Pharisee If . . .

A Pharisee is hard on others and easy on himself, but
a spiritual man is easy on others and hard on himself.

~ A. W. Tozer

Even though it's been "a long time ago in a galaxy far, far
away" since Pharisees were running around in Century One
causing trouble for God's messengers, Pharisees and Pharisaism are still here.

They're like the poor. *They'll always be with you.*

While Pharisaism is in sharp decline today (experiencing
advanced stages of rigor mortis), the pharisaic spirit still exists. And it's the chief reason why so many non-Christians
want nothing to do with Jesus.

When I was eighteen years old, I spent a lot of time in a
group that bred Pharisees like rabbits. And I will shamefully
admit that I was one of them.

Thank God, however, I experienced the washing machine of life and it drained much (or all, hopefully) of the Pharisee out of me. Regrettably, that doesn't happen with everyone. Many Christians waste their sufferings. And so they remain just as hardened, callous, self-righteous, and judgmental as they were in their youth.

That said, you just might be a modern-day Pharisee if . . .

You hate people who sin differently than you do.

(Isn't it ironic that God hates the same people Pharisees do?) *Cough.*

Jesus said to beware of the leaven of the Pharisees, which is hypocrisy. Pharisees play the sin-metrics game. Magnifying the sins of others while not even wincing at your own.

Regrettably, "Christian" Pharisees produce more vitriol and spread more poison than a Chernobyl-like nuclear disaster. Dispensing slander is labeled "poison" by the Bible because it exposes innocent souls to toxic substances which are spiritually lethal.

Pharisees are adept at vilification, bombing others "with God on their side."

You wake up with criticism in your heart, plotting against those you wish to destroy, even before the coffee gets cold.

In this regard, Pharisees minister toxicity and death to those who love God (all in the name of God).

For a leaven-dispensing Pharisee, it's shoot first, ask questions later. The exact opposite of what James as well as Jesus told us, for that matter (James 1:19; 4:11; Matthew 7:1–4, 12).

As E. Stanley Jones rightly pointed out, "The measure of my spirit of criticism is the measure of my distance from Christ."[1]

You seem incapable of apologizing—sincerely, that is.

It breaks a Pharisee's jaw to admit he's wrong or apologize to those he's mistreated. You'll have a better chance seeing a hen floss her teeth than to witness a Pharisee apologizing or admitting to a mistake.

In this regard, Pharisees exhibit a remarkable lack of self-awareness.

This also accounts for why they are so belligerent. They exist to correct others, never turning the spotlight inward.

You only hang out with other Pharisees.

Because Pharisees establish dubious doctrinal criteria by which every Christian is judged and condemned to hell, they hang only with their own kind.

In addition, they aren't a terribly happy bunch of people. They weren't in Jesus' day either. In one Greek manuscript, they are called "lemon suckers." (Okay, I made that up. But it's not far off the mark.)

You impute evil motives to the hearts of others (then call it "discernment").

Pharisees are clueless to the fact that they betray their own hearts whenever they judge the heart of another. Because Pharisees have anointed themselves to be the guardians of "biblical purity," there is always some enemy to fight.

They also engage in the usual fare of claiming to uphold "Christian values" while they paper over the harmful things they've done in the name of Jesus—unfairly sitting over others in judgment.

NEWSFLASH: Only God has the ability to read the motives of mortals. And as I've contended elsewhere, the New Testament has zero tolerance when humans engage in it.

You cannot tolerate correction, even when it's given in the spirit of Christ.

A Pharisee hasn't caught on to the fact that everyone has blind spots, including herself. Pharisees are quick to join the bandwagon of brother/sister bashing, leveraging rhetorical bullying tactics claiming that God is on their side.

For the Pharisee, reacting in the flesh and vilifying others is an art form. They are adept at crafting special attacks against those who don't line up with their unique interpretations of Scripture. And they break out in boils whenever someone points out their own flaws.

As Len Sweet and I argued in *Jesus: A Theography*, the things that make Jesus angry aren't what most evangelicals get angry about.

Concluding Point

I suspect that as you were reading this chapter, your brain was populating with different people who fit my description of a Pharisee.

But that's not really the intent. Sometimes we need to turn those rifle scopes into mirrors and ask ourselves, does any of this describe me?

In which case, repentance—a U-turn of the heart—is the cure.

Sadly for many, conscience is that still small voice that tells you what other people should do.

By the way, intelligence has nothing to do with the insidious danger of Pharisaism. Some modern-day Pharisees are freakishly smart. But that doesn't count for much in God's eyes (see 1 Corinthians 1 and 2).

It's time to move past our fears in the name of "protecting theological boundaries" and with grace and humility join the conversation that's been going on for centuries.

When it comes to God's family, there is no place for erecting walls of isolation and narrowing the borders of who is in and who is out. In this regard, Pharisaism replaces the divine dream with a human nightmare.

Alas, the heavens are darkened by our refusal to love each other.

May God be merciful to us all.

17

Twenty Reasons Why
the Christian Right
and the Christian Left
Won't Adopt Me

You can be straight as a gun barrel theologically and
just as empty as one spiritually.

~ A. W. Tozer

In April 2012, I wrote a blog post using the title of this chapter. The post went viral. It seemed to have hit a nerve as well as give language to how countless Christians around the world feel about the incessant bickering over doctrinal and political issues among God's people.

I'm including it here because I believe it sums up the main point of this book.

Why the Christian Right Won't Adopt Me

- Like F. F. Bruce, I believe words like *plenary* and *inerrant* are unnecessary when speaking about the truthfulness of Scripture.
- I don't believe the Bible clearly addresses the question of the eternal destiny of those who have never heard or understood the gospel of Jesus Christ.
- I don't believe Scripture answers every question posed to it. And there are many questions, including theological ones, which are shrouded in mystery.
- I believe that racism and sexism are serious problems in the USA and shouldn't be viewed as "lesser" than other moral evils.
- I believe that slander, hatred, greed, and fits of rage are just as sinful as fornication and stealing (so did Paul—1 Corinthians 6:10–11; Galatians 5:19–21).
- I don't know whether to whistle or wind my watch, to laugh or cry at *The American Patriot's Bible*.
- I believe that God loves the poor and taking care of them should be just as high a priority as other social issues, if not more.
- While I don't believe the theory of evolution with respect to human origins is airtight, many genuine and devout Christians (past and present) believe it to be fact ("theistic evolution"). And because Christ has received them, so do I.

- I believe a narrative approach to the Bible is a far superior way to understand Scripture than a systematic approach.
- While I disagree with him on many things, I find some of what Brian McLaren teaches to be valuable.

Why the Christian Left Won't Adopt Me

- I believe the Bible—all of it—is divinely inspired, completely true, fully authoritative, and wholly reliable.
- I believe that when Jesus said He is the Way, the Truth, and the Life and no man comes to the Father but by Him, He wasn't lying. Nor was He being narrow-minded. (And I believe Jesus of Nazareth actually uttered those words.)
- Though I possess neither, I don't believe it is a sin to own a Cadillac Escalade or a private jet.
- I believe that accusing people of racism and sexism when they aren't racist or sexist is just as wrong as racism and sexism.
- I sometimes think there is too much talk about rights and not enough talk about taking responsibility.
- I believe that Paul's words about work in 2 Thessalonians 3:10–12 still hold true today.
- Postmodern deconstructionism, while helpful in discounting modernity (whose fundamental tenets challenge Christianity), is inadequate for bringing one to the Truth, who is Christ.

- I believe there is a big difference between the world system and the ekklesia; and the former is God's enemy (1 John 2:15–17).
- There are still many first-rate scholars who argue that there are sound historical and scientific reasons for believing that Adam was a real, historical person. And it is wrong to ridicule and scorn them.
- While I disagree with him on many things, I find some of what John MacArthur teaches to be valuable.

The Family to Which I Belong

Note that I could easily lengthen the list and expand each point.

Of course, not everyone who aligns themselves with the Christian Right affirms each point I've listed above. Yet many do. The same is true for those who align themselves with the Christian Left. Yet many do.

And just for good measure, I don't believe in making a fetish out of political or theological centrism.

That said, it's okay if the Christian Left and the Christian Right movements won't adopt me. You see, I belong to the Family of God, which is made up of all who have the Lord's life within them. And that includes my sisters and brothers in Christ who are on the left and the right.

It may surprise some that I have close friends and family members who are on the far right on the political and theological spectrum, and they are intensely and passionately involved in the political process.

I also have close friends and family members who are on the far left on the political and theological spectrum, and they are intensely and passionately involved in the political process.

I'm glad they are following their vision, conscience, and passion, as I believe all believers should.

Let me say two things parenthetically at this point:

(1) It's fascinating to me that people who are part of the Christian Left and the Christian Right routinely accuse one another of accommodating the culture and supporting Caesar and Empire.

(2) As a generality, the Left believes in speaking to "power." However, when it does, it's usually in the areas of contra racism, alleviating poverty, protesting against unjust war, etc. In general, the Right also believes in speaking to "power." However, when it does, it's usually in the areas of the fight against abortion, pornography, and other moral issues.

Very rarely do we see leaders or movements today in the spirit of Joseph Cardinal Bernardin, who advocated "the seamless garment," protesting against abortion as well as the causes which produce poverty and unjust war. To Bernardin, to fight against abortion, war, poverty, and the death penalty was to be consistently pro-life.

Let me add a postscript: Being a liberal Democrat doesn't make one "cool" any more than being a conservative Republican makes one "moral." So it seems to me anyway.

End of parenthetical statement.

Again, I've always encouraged Christians to follow their vision, conscience, and passion regarding what they believe God's will is for the world. And I applaud believers who are laboring in the trenches with respect to God's kingdom work. As I've written and spoken elsewhere, such work is important to me, and it's something in which I'm actively engaged myself.

For that reason, while I may disagree with my friends and family members on various theological, social, and political points, we love, respect, and support one another. Especially in the work of helping those who are needy and suffering, both on the justice side and on the mercy side.

And our differences have never affected our relationship.

So even if the Right and Left movements won't adopt me, I happily declare that I am kin to all genuine followers of Jesus, regardless of their political or theological bent.

And they will know we are Christians by our love for one another.

> They drew a circle that shut me out—a heretic, rebel, a thing to flout. But love and I had the wit to win. We drew a circle that took them in.
>
> ~ Edwin Markham

The Loss of Civility

In closing, I really appreciate what Rick Warren said in an interview with ABC News:

> The coarsening of our culture and the loss of civility in our civilization is one of the things that concerns me most about our nation. We don't know how to disagree without being

disagreeable. The fact is, you can—you can walk hand in hand without seeing eye-to-eye. And what we need in our country is unity, not uniformity. There are major differences, politically, religiously, economically in our nation. We have many different streams in our nation. . . . What is solvable is how we treat each other with our differences. . . . In fact, the Bible tells me in 1 Peter, show respect to everyone, even people I totally disagree with. So I'm coming from that viewpoint in that we must return civility to our civilization in order to get on. But the reason I do that is because of the deeper reason, there's a spiritual root to my reason for civility.[1]

18

So You Think You Disagree?

Men often stumble over the truth, but most pick themselves up and hurry on as if nothing happened.

~ Winston Churchill

If you have ever had someone disagree with something you've
said or written . . . or you've disagreed with what someone
has ever said or written, then this chapter is for you.

Three things by way of introduction. When people disagree with you . . .

- Some will be charitable in their disagreement.
- Others will be defamatory.
- Sometimes many of the people who think they disagree with you *really* don't. But because "Christians"
  often fail to do that which Jesus taught—which is to
  go straight to the person with whom you *think* you

disagree and ask them questions—misrepresentations abound (Matthew 7:12).

To be sure, there are genuine disagreements. And we should welcome them. It's one way to fine-tune our thinking. None of us can claim infallibility.

But in all the years that I've been writing books, blogging, and speaking, I've discovered that after having a respectful conversation with a reasonable person, we often learn that there is no substantive disagreement.

In my experience at least, this happens approximately 75 percent of the time.

That said, here are four reasons why a person may think they disagree with you when they really don't. Note that I'm using the word "author" here to refer to the human source of *any* piece of writing or speech.

1. The author wasn't clear in making his point, so his points were misunderstood.

When it comes to articulating our thoughts, we all have room for improvement. For myself, I'm constantly honing my writing, restating things, rewording sentences, nuancing ideas, and reworking my material to be as clear as possible. Yet I'm rarely satisfied with what I've written. Winston Churchill perfectly describes my experience when he said,

> Writing a book is an adventure. To begin with, it is a toy and an amusement; then it becomes a mistress, and then it becomes a master, and then a tyrant. The last phase is that just as you are about to be reconciled to your servitude, you kill the monster, and fling him out to the public.

Sometimes, our words lend themselves to misunderstanding. In such cases, there is no substantive disagreement, just a misunderstanding.

Takeaway: Ask the author for clarification if you think you may be misunderstanding him or her.

2. The author's statements have been taken out of context and misrepresented, then spread to others.

This happens more than you know.

The little red book that I wrote with George Barna in 2008 is reported to be "the most reviewed book by those who've never read it."*

This provoked us to create a special Q&A page for readers on PaganChristianity.org where we respond to objections and critiques. Potential readers can clearly see what we say in the book and what we don't say.

Unfortunately, some people will *intentionally* misrepresent another person's words. One sure sign of this is when a person criticizes a work, but they won't post a clickable link to the source they are criticizing. This is done so that those reading the critique cannot easily check to see if the critique is accurate or not. (This is especially true for online blogs, audios, and articles.)

Takeaway: If someone critiques a piece of writing or talk, be sure to read or listen to the object of the critique yourself. This way you will know if the critique is accurate or not.

---

*Referencing Frank Viola and George Barna, *Pagan Christianity* (Carol Stream, IL: Tyndale, 2008). The misrepresentations surrounding that book were so outlandish that they would make *Star Trek*'s Mr. Spock blush. (That's saying something, because Spock has seen everything in the universe.)

Never believe a negative critique without first reading the actual source that's being critiqued. Even if there are direct quotations in the critique, that doesn't make it accurate. Quotations are like sound bytes that can be easily taken out of context. People do this when misrepresenting the Bible all the time.

3. The author's statements are filtered through the reader's experience.

Sometimes people read their own experiences and assumptions into what they read and hear. The net effect is that the intended meaning the author had in mind is changed.

Take the word *prophetic*, for instance. Some people understand that word to mean God directly gives an individual His exact words. Others understand it to mean a challenging word in the style of the Old Testament prophets. Others view it as a word that reveals Jesus Christ. Others understand it to be a word that predicts the future.

See what I mean? Words like *organic*, *missional*, and *church* are routinely used to mean very different things by many different people.

Takeaway: Find out what an author means by a certain word before drawing a conclusion.

4. The author's statements are misunderstood due to a differing spiritual conversational style.

In *Revise Us Again*, I introduce readers to the three main spiritual conversational styles. Ever try talking spirituality or theology with another Christian who uses a different spiritual conversational style than you? The result: *popcorn.* People think they disagree when they really don't. Your discussion was shanghaied by a differing conversation style.*

Takeaway: Recognize that your disagreement may be rooted in a differing conversational style.

A Word to Readers

Again, I repeat this important point: If you read a critique that disturbs or concerns you, always, always, always go directly to the source that's being critiqued. *Read the original work yourself.* And if necessary, ask the author directly what she or he believes.

A Word to Writers

If you are a writer who is turning the sod on an issue, you and your work *will* be misrepresented at some point.

How you react, however, reveals volumes about your spiritual stature.

I've watched too many authors and bloggers return fire on those who attack them or misrepresent their work. This is the way of the flesh and shows nothing of the cross of Jesus Christ.

Trust the Lord with the matter. In most cases, those who are discerning will go to bat for you and defend your work. You don't have to defend yourself. Let God do the defending.

Taking the high road, the road of our Lord Jesus, often means remaining silent when under attack.

---

*This point differs from the previous one in that conversational styles are about *how* one communicates over against the *meaning* one ascribes to certain words.

To this you were called, because Christ suffered for you, leaving you an example, that you should follow in his steps. "He committed no sin, and no deceit was found in his mouth." When they hurled their insults at him, he did not retaliate; when he suffered, he made no threats. Instead, he entrusted himself to him who judges justly. (1 Peter 2:21–23)

In addition, as a writer, you should make yourself accessible to your readers. Even if it's through a personal assistant. Inaccessibility is the outstanding trait of the celebrity. Try writing to Kim Kardashian or Justin Bieber and getting a response. The same holds true for some Christian authors today. *Not that there's anything wrong with that* (to quote Seinfeld) . . . if being a celebrity is the way you want to roll.

But in my judgment, for a Christian leader, you should be accessible to answer questions about your work from people who are open-minded, think the best of you, and genuinely want to understand what you're saying. Not just for their sake, but also for your own. (Trolls are the exception, of course. Never feed them.)

19

The Art of Being a Jerk Online

The difference between you and God is that God doesn't think He's you.

~ Anne Lamott

If you're past the age of Mosaics and Busters, you might want to make sure you're sitting down. In fact, you may want to hold on to your chair real tight. I'm using a style of language here that some may misinterpret. I'm doing it to make a point. So "Frankie says relax" before you read on . . .

Jerk: Slang. a contemptibly naive, fatuous, foolish, or inconsequential person.

It's not a cuss word.

According to recent studies (you know, the same ones that show that research is known to cause cancer in rats), if two Christians disagree with one another online for more than three consecutive days, there is a 97.3 percent chance that one of them will end up calling the other a "child of Satan" or a near equivalent.

With that in mind, here are ten surefire ways to perfect the art of being a jerk online.

1. Move from arguing the substance of a disagreement to attacking the person with whom you disagree.

This is called an ad hominem argument. Attack the messenger when you disagree with his message. People often do this when they can't win an argument.

Example: "I just read your view on the atonement of Christ. You are a first-class heretic, obviously someone who has a black heart. In fact, my discernment tells me that you are the spawn of Satan. May God have mercy on your soul!"

2. Assume what other people think and believe rather than asking them directly.

And state your assumption about what they think and believe as though it were gospel fact to others. (Too many Christians assume what other people believe without actually going to them and asking. I'm always amazed when Christians do this.)

3. Write things to or about your fellow sistas and bruthas in Christ that you would never have the gall to say to their faces.

In other words, play the part of a gutless wonder and a spineless coward.

4. Don't read a blog post or comment carefully.

Instead, read "into it," jump to conclusions, then go off (or go snarky) on the blogger or commenter. To be more specific, never ask clarifying questions about something you just read (such as, "Maybe I'm not understanding you correctly, but are you saying xyz?" . . . or "If what you're saying is true, what is your response to abc?"). Nope. Just lay into the person after you've "read into" their post or comment. Ask no questions in a gracious manner, only make statements and accusations.

5. Write something online when you are angry or your feelings have just been hurt.

Give no time to bring it to the Lord. Stone that angel who is telling you to wait because you're not in the Spirit. Instead, let your emotions control your reaction.

6. Presume to know what another person is thinking and assume you know the motives behind their words and actions.

Put yourself in the seat that only God Almighty occupies and impugn their intentions. (Anytime a person says something like, "You said that because" . . . or "You were trying to xyz when you said or did abc," that person is judging the motives of another mortal.)

7. Engage in "drive-by" character assassination by posting a comment on other people's blogs that smears the reputation of another child of God.

Don't post your real name and your real email address when you leave the flaming comment. And hope that the blogger is sloppy enough not to notice the comment so they don't delete it immediately. (As heinous and immature as this is, I'm sorry to say that some "Christians" actually do this sort of thing. Interestingly, every comment left on a blog has an identifiable IP address. So it's not that difficult to identify the person.)

8. If someone gives you a response, ignore their response and repeat your points over again.

Have the attitude, "Don't confuse me with the facts," and disregard what they say. Just keep pushing the same points over and over again, hoping they will eventually agree with you.

9. With forethought and deliberation, completely misrepresent what another person has said or written, then play the victim.

For instance, accuse someone of attacking others when they've attacked no one. Accuse them of holding to beliefs and ideas that they don't hold to. Play on the fact that some Christians will believe whatever you write instead of going to the source to verify the accuracy of what you're saying.

While this is the height of fleshly activity, it's fitting for the one who is perfecting the art of being an online jerk.

10. Forget what your Lord taught you.

Defy your spiritual instincts and grieve the Holy Spirit of God by treating other people (especially those you don't like) in a way that you would never want to be treated yourself. Post things online to and about others that you'd never want posted to and about you or your loved ones. In other words, claim you believe Jesus' words in Matthew 7:12, but disobey them without flinching.

20

Warning: The World Is Watching How We Christians Treat One Another

> If Christians cannot extend grace through faithful presence within the body of believers, they will not be able to extend grace to those outside.
>
> ~ James Davison Hunter

Recently, someone asked me the following question:

Frank, if I had to summarize your ministry, it would be that Jesus is more than we ever imagined and we can learn to live by His life which is evidenced by treating others the same way we want to be treated. Would you say that this is accurate?

My answer:

Yes, that sums it up well. These two themes are underscored in many of my books and blog posts.

Several years ago, I wrote a piece for a periodical explaining why I am a Christian. I ended the piece by asking why those who aren't Christians have decided not to follow Jesus (yet, at least). Here's what one person wrote:

> I'm not a Christian because of how most of the Christians I've known treat each other. Not loving like their founder taught but just the opposite. I like that your list wasn't apologetic or combative but personal and I respect that. Rare but nice to see.

This harkens back to Gandhi's famous line,

> I like your Christ, I do not like your Christians. Your Christians are so unlike your Christ. . . . If it weren't for Christians, I'd be a Christian.

Take a look at this graphic which shows how people search on Google for "Christians" in comparison to "Muslims" and "Jews." (Credit goes to my friend John Saddington for this analysis.)

This graphic shows some of the serious stereotypes that we Christians are up against. Unfortunately, the stereotypes are often painfully true.

It's not uncommon for some Christians to throw verbal assaults at one another on Facebook, blogs, Twitter, and other internet venues. As a result, the world sees people who profess to follow Jesus—the Prince of Peace—fighting, misrepresenting one another, and even "blocking" one another.

> But if you bite and devour one another, watch out that you are not consumed by one another. (Galatians 5:15 ESV)

why are muslims so

why are muslims so **violent**
why are muslims so **stupid**
why are muslims so **angry**
why are muslims so **crazy**
why are muslims so **sensitive**
why are muslims so **hateful**
why are muslims so **intolerant**
why are muslims so **backward**
why are muslims so **evil**
why are muslims so **extreme**

Google Search

why are jews so

why are jews so **cheap**
why are jews so **successful**
why are jews so **smart**
why are jews so **rich**
why are jews so **greedy**
why are jews so **annoying**
why are jews so **hated**
why are jews so **ugly**
why are jews so **liberal**
why are jews so **funny**

Google Search

why are christians so

why are christians so **stupid**
why are christians so **judgmental**
why are christians so **ignorant**
why are christians so **hateful**
why are christians so **intolerant**
why are christians so **mean**
why are christians so **narrow minded**
why are christians so **hypocritical**
why are christians so **annoying**
why are christians so **crazy**

Google Search

why are buddhists so

why are buddhists so **happy**

Google Search

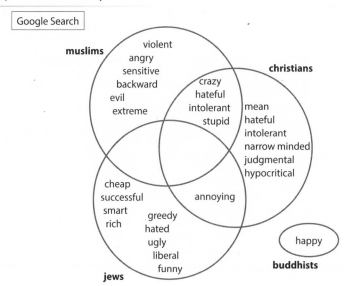

There once were two cats of Kilkenny
Each thought there was one cat too many
So they fought and they fit
And they scratched and they bit
'Til excepting their nails
And the tips of their tails
Instead of two cats there weren't any.

Civil disagreement and even debate, when done in the spirit of Christ, are healthy and helpful.

But when disagreements descend into second-guessing motives, distortions of one another's words, mischaracterizations of one another's views, and personal attacks, then we've moved into the flesh.

The net is that the name of Jesus gets tarnished in no small way.

So how do we change that?

Here are seven points to consider the next time you think you have a possible disagreement with another Christian.

1. Go to them privately and *ask* them what they *meant* by what they said, did, or wrote or what they *allegedly* said, did, or wrote.

Jesus said to go to our brother or sister in private if we have an issue with them. Since we don't want to misrepresent others in public, going to them directly helps prevent this. And you would want the same treatment if the shoe happened to be on your foot.

About six months ago, I was reading someone's Facebook wall where they quoted a friend of mine who came out with a new book on evangelism. The entire thread was about what my friend *may* have meant or didn't mean. People got angry at one another. Some began blocking others. (These are Christians, mind you.)*

Finally, a woman jumped in and said, "Excuse me, but instead of questioning what he may have meant or didn't mean, why don't you just write him a message and ask him? He's on Facebook, you know."

Her remark arrested everyone and you could smell the embarrassment. Amazingly, no one ever thought to even try to contact my friend and ask. If they had done so in the beginning, the whole issue would have been resolved and the carnage wouldn't have even begun.

2. When you go to another believer privately, ask them questions. Don't make accusations.

Again, put yourself in their shoes and ask yourself, "How would I want to be treated if this person was me and I had concerns or possible problems with them?" In my experience, I've found that accusations based on second- or thirdhand information are usually inaccurate. And they are often rooted in misunderstandings.

One time Jesus made a statement about one of His followers, saying,

"If I want him to remain alive until I return, what is that to you? You must follow me." Because of this remark, a rumor

---

*My editor was concerned that some of my readers wouldn't know what "blocking" someone on social media is. So for those of you who are reading this book in the twenty-second century, to block someone on social media means that they cannot see your social media updates. You are invisible to them and they to you.

spread among the disciples that the disciple Jesus was referring to would never die. But Jesus never said that this disciple would not die; He only said, "If I want him to remain alive until I return, what is that to you?" (John 21:22–23)

If Jesus—the perfect Teacher—was misunderstood by those who were in His corner, how much more does it happen with us?

3. Never, ever, evah, nevah judge the motives or intentions of another human being. To do so is to sin against them and against God.

You and I cannot read someone else's heart. While it's fine to question someone's judgment, it's wrong to judge their motives. Love "thinks no evil," Paul said in 1 Corinthians 13 (NKJV), but it always believes the best of others. Again, this is covered under Jesus' gold-plated "do unto others" commandment.

4. Never entertain gossip or slander about another sister or brother in Christ.

Again, treat others the same way you want them to treat you. Jesus not only commanded this, He said this commandment fulfills the Law and the Prophets (Matthew 7:12). By the way, I've found that many Christians don't know what slander or gossip is (unless it's happening to them). They mistakenly think that if something is true or half true, it's not gossip or slander.*

*For a superb article on the biblical meaning of gossip and slander, see frank viola.org/slander.

5. Seek peace with all you have. "If it is possible, as far as it depends on you, live at peace with everyone," Paul said in Romans 12:18.

We aren't going to agree on everything. In fact, I am unaware of any book that exists where all Christians agree with every word or understand every word the same way. That includes the Bible itself.

So we should be open for correction. But how you approach someone is incredibly important. *How we treat one another while we disagree is just as important as the nature of our disagreement.*

6. Remember that the world is watching how we Christians treat one another and talk about one another.

You can be the greatest evangelist on planet Earth in terms of being able to boldly witness to non-Christians about Jesus. And you can blow the loudest trumpet about mission and discipleship. But if you treat your fellow sisters and brothers in Christ in ways that you would never want to be treated yourself, then you nullify your evangelistic efforts. In addition, how you treat your fellow brothers and sisters is monumentally important to our Lord.

7. Remember Jesus' last prayer on earth before He gave His life for us.

It gives us a peek into what's foremost in His heart.

My prayer is not for them alone. I pray also for those who will believe in me through their message, that all of them may be one, Father, just as you are in me and I am in you. May they also be in us so that the world may believe that you have sent me. (John 17:20–21)

21

Misrepresentations

People understand me so poorly that they don't even understand my complaint about them not understanding me.

~ Søren Kierkegaard

It's common courtesy in the academic world to send a manuscript which critiques someone else's work to the author of that work before the manuscript is published and circulated (via a blog, magazine article, or book).

The reason is simple. Intellectual honesty demands accuracy in the critique. It's important to truthfully and fairly represent someone's work when critiquing it. Without such, straw-man arguments get passed off as honest critiques. This breeds the misrepresentation of a person's work (which is largely exacerbated by the internet, which is noted for making misinformation viral).

One of the lessons God has taught me is that He sovereignly uses misrepresentation for His own purposes. It's yet another case of God doing what He's so good at—writing straight with crooked lines.*

So if you are an author who is breaking with status quo thinking or practice, you would be wise to accept misrepresentations as coming from the hand of your Lord.

Sometimes the Lord uses such misrepresentations to keep certain people from reading a book or hearing a message at a certain time in their lives. Perhaps at those times when they are not ready to receive it.

Other times it is to humble the person whose work is being misrepresented. Sometimes it's to give opportunity to demonstrate to others how to accept criticism and unfair critiques, handling them with grace and refusing to attack back or defend oneself.

Still other times it's to magnify the truth. When a person must resort to misrepresentation and/or ad hominem (personal attacks) to discredit a spiritual statement, it only underscores the truth of that statement.

In July 2010, an ex-pastor in his thirties visited me. We had breakfast together, and he told me a fascinating story. He said that when he was serving as a pastor, he kept hearing about *Pagan Christianity*.

But he was told not to read it, that it was just an attack on Christmas and Easter and other trivial matters. So he had no interest in looking at it.

---

*Unfortunately, many contemporary Christians have never been taught about the principle of the cross and how God uses suffering and mistreatment to accomplish His purpose in transforming us into His image. For a discussion on this neglected aspect of biblical teaching, see my books *God's Favorite Place on Earth* (Colorado Springs: David C. Cook, 2013) and *From Eternity to Here* (Colorado Springs: David C. Cook, 2009).

Yet every time he would pray, strangely, the title kept coming to his mind. Time passed and one day he was at Barnes and Noble. Before entering into the store, he asked God what book he should buy and read (he had done this before— praying about what book to buy and read before entering a bookstore).

As he walked through the Christian section, he saw *Pagan Christianity* staring him in the face, and he intuitively knew he should buy it.

Upon reading it, it wasn't anything like he had thought or heard. There wasn't a word in it about Christmas or Easter, for example. All told, he said the book changed his life and put him on a brand-new journey with the Lord and His ultimate intention.

Beware the person who quotes short excerpts from a book and then purports to interpret the author of the book. In many (if not most) cases where the interpretation is negative, the person is misrepresenting the author. You'll also discover something else in virtually every case—the person quoting and interpreting has never gone to the author to ask if she is understanding the author correctly.

Point: If you think you disagree with an author, go to the author directly and ask if you are understanding her or him correctly before you make your views public. Intellectual honesty demands it.

To my mind, this act alone would remove 95 percent of the misrepresentations that abound in the Christian community today.

22

Possessing a Mind to Suffer

One of the Lord's apostles wrote these remarkable words:

> Therefore, since Christ suffered in his body, arm yourselves also with the same attitude, because whoever suffers in the body is done with sin. As a result, they do not live the rest of their earthly lives for evil human desires, but rather for the will of God. (1 Peter 4:1–2)

Suffering is a big topic in the New Testament, but it's largely overlooked today. No one wants to hear that the Christian life holds everything for you that it held for Jesus Christ, including His sufferings.

Nonetheless, those who will grow in Christ have learned how to be run over, be taken advantage of, be stapled, bent, folded, and mutilated.

The resolve in their hearts has been, "They can string me up, nail me, scalp me, quarter me, burn me, scatter my ashes and do a happy dance over them. But I still won't recant my faith in Jesus Christ or His Word. Nor will I retaliate in kind."

Many of our forefathers of the faith possessed this resolve. They had a mind to suffer, and they did in the most violent ways.

While those who live in the West right now will rarely experience physical persecution for their devotion to Christ, they will often receive verbal—and cyber—persecution.

And sadly, the shipment of nails will be delivered to their door from fellow "Christians"—usually out of jealousy or a doctrinal difference.

> Yea, and all that will live godly in Christ Jesus shall suffer persecution. (2 Timothy 3:12 KJV)

Thus part of regracing is to possess an attitude to suffer (1 Peter 4:1).

23

The Essentials of Our Faith

I will not quarrel with you about my opinions; only see that your heart is right toward God, that you know and love the Lord Jesus Christ; that you love your neighbor, and walk as your Master walked, and I desire no more. I am sick of opinions; am weary to bear them; my soul loathes this frosty food. Give me solid and substantial religion; give me a humble, gentle lover of God and man; a man full of mercy and good faith, without partiality and without hypocrisy; a man laying himself out in the work of faith, the patience of hope, the labor of love. Let my soul be with these Christians wheresoever they are, and whatsoever opinion they are of.

~ John Wesley

There's a question that my readers ask me all the time. (Truthfully, they rarely ask me anything, because who cares what I think. But let's keep up the pretense.)

My readers ask me all the time what the essentials of the Christian faith are—you know, those beliefs that tell us who is in and who is out of the kingdom of God.

A seventeenth-century quote, which has been wrongly attributed to Augustine, goes like this:

> In essentials unity, in non-essentials liberty, in all things charity.[1]

But what are the essentials of the faith and what does one do when someone violates them?

C. S. Lewis defined the essentials of the faith as "the belief that has been common to nearly all Christians at all times."[2]

An earlier version of the same idea was put forth by Vincent of Lérins in these words: "Christianity is what has been held always, everywhere, and by all."

In *Reimagining Church*, I set forth the authority of the Scriptures as being the unchangeable standard for Christian faith and practice—including church practice. In the course of that book, I also discuss the creeds of the Christian faith, saying,

> Historic Christian teaching on the essential doctrines of the faith plays a crucial role in keeping a church on scriptural track. Throughout the centuries, Christians have preserved the core beliefs of our faith: Jesus Christ is God and man, He was born of a virgin, He was crucified for our sins, He rose again in bodily form, etc.
>
> These core beliefs do not belong to any one ecclesiastical tradition or denomination. Instead, they are the heritage of all genuine believers. And they reflect the voice of the church throughout history. These "essentials of the faith"

embody what C. S. Lewis called Mere Christianity—"the belief that has been common to nearly all Christians at all times."

Thus the call to recover the ecology of the New Testament church doesn't translate into a summons to reinvent the religious wheel on every theological issue. Nor does it include a rejection of all that has been passed down to us by our spiritual forefathers. At the same time, everything that is postapostolic is subject to scrutiny and should be critiqued by the apostolic tradition itself.

The call to restore organic Christianity sides with every voice of the past that has remained true to apostolic revelation—no matter what segment of the historic church to which they may have belonged. The primitive church was rooted in the soil of Christian truth. And staying within that soil requires that we stand on the shoulders of those who have gone before us. As C. H. Spurgeon affirmed, "I intend to grasp tightly with one hand the truths I have already learned, and to keep the other hand wide open to take in the things I do not yet know."[3]

Ever since the fourth century, Christians have divided the body of Christ over peripheral doctrines. In this regard, the seamless coat of Christ has been unnecessarily rent.

On the other hand, there are doctrines that form the pillars of our faith, and some who "are not serving Christ our Lord" and use "smooth talk and glowing words" deceive the innocent by contradicting those teachings (Romans 16:18 NLT). Or as Peter put it,

> But there were also false prophets among the people, just as there will be false teachers among you. They will secretly introduce destructive heresies, even denying the sovereign

Lord who bought them—bringing swift destruction on themselves. (2 Peter 2:1)

What, then, are these pillars of the Christian faith?

What follows are the Apostles' Creed and the Nicene Creed—two creeds I believe all Christians should be familiar with as they are part of our heritage.

While these creeds aren't *complete* theological statements, they are *correct* theological statements. And they represent the consensus of the body of Christ throughout the ages.

So while the language is archaic and the content isn't exhaustive, the meaning is accurate.

Oh, and while we are on the topic, my fiercest critics are people who reject the authority and reliability of the Scriptures as well as rejecting my affirmation of the Christian creeds. But I will not recant on either as I have yet to see compelling evidence to overturn them.

Here they are . . .

The Apostles' Creed

I believe in God, the Father almighty, creator of heaven and earth.

I believe in Jesus Christ, God's only Son, our Lord, who was conceived by the Holy Spirit, born of the Virgin Mary, suffered under Pontius Pilate, was crucified, died, and was buried; he descended into hell.

On the third day he rose again; he ascended into heaven, he is seated at the right hand of the Father, and he will come again to judge the living and the dead.

I believe in the Holy Spirit, the holy universal church, the communion of saints, the forgiveness of sins, the resurrection of the body, and the life everlasting. Amen.

The Nicene Creed

I believe in one God, the Father Almighty, Maker of heaven and earth, and of all things visible and invisible.

And in one Lord Jesus Christ, the only-begotten Son of God, begotten of the Father before all worlds; God of God, Light of Light, very God of very God; begotten, not made, being of one substance with the Father, by whom all things were made.

Who, for us men and for our salvation, came down from heaven, and was incarnate by the Holy Spirit of the virgin Mary, and was made man; and was crucified also for us under Pontius Pilate; He suffered and was buried; and the third day He rose again, according to the Scriptures; and ascended into heaven, and sits on the right hand of the Father; and He shall come again, with glory, to judge the quick and the dead; whose kingdom shall have no end.

And I believe in the Holy Ghost, the Lord and Giver of Life; who proceeds from the Father and the Son; who with the Father and the Son together is worshiped and glorified; who spoke by the prophets.

And I believe in one holy universal and apostolic church. I acknowledge one baptism for the remission of sins; and I look for the resurrection of the dead, and the life of the world to come. Amen.

Despite that these two creeds are imperfect, archaic statements, they rightfully set forth the orthodox tenets of the Christian faith. For example, the divinity of Jesus Christ, His death for our sins, His bodily resurrection.

How, then, should we treat a person who denies any of these "essentials" of the faith? Should we impale them? Should we verbally peel their hide, make them walk the plank, or shun them?

May I offer a proposal?

How about treating them the same way *you* wish to be treated if you were in their shoes (Matthew 7:12)? That includes gently correcting them, realizing that we ourselves only come to the knowledge of the truth by God's grace.

Three additional points to ponder on this score.

1. The failure to understand a biblical doctrine isn't the same as outright denying it. Often, when someone denies a scriptural truth, the reason is because they've never been taught properly about it. So instead of reacting with "Slaughter the villains! Off with their heads!"— how about trying to explain "the way of God more accurately" to them (Acts 18:26 NASB)?

2. It's more important to God to be Christlike than it is to be doctrinally right. Because if you're not Christlike, you're not right, even if you have all your theological ducks in a row (2 Timothy 2:24–25).

3. Don't make the common mistake of condemning a person through "guilt by association." Just because an author may mention or even quote another author doesn't at all mean that the first author agrees with all

the viewpoints of the author they are mentioning or quoting.

All told, if a person denies a biblical tenet of the faith and begins pushing their false views onto others—thus causing division—that's another story. The biblical term for this is *heresy*, which we'll explore in our next chapter.

24

Who Are the Real Heretics?

It's the mathematician that goes mad, not the poet.

~ G. K. Chesterton

This chapter was originally published on my blog. The blog post was entitled "Read This Before You Drop the H-Bomb on a Fellow Christian." And it was written with Greg Boyd.

"Heretic." It's a favorite word that many Christians have no problem dropping on the heads of their fellow sisters and brothers.

In common parlance, the term is used to describe any person who disagrees with "orthodox Christian teaching." The problem, of course, is that there are different perspectives on what exactly constitutes "orthodox Christian teaching."

Some claim this for Calvinism, while others claim this for Arminianism or for Roman Catholicism or for Eastern Orthodoxy.

And we must not forget the many fundamentalist groups who reserve the term *orthodox* only for people who agree with every one of their distinctive beliefs and/or practices.

Two thousand years down the church history pike and the body of Christ is sliced and diced into over 33,000 fragments, some of which pull the heresy lever on everyone else without blinking.

In this essay, we are definitely not going to suggest that false teaching doesn't exist. It existed at the time of Jesus and Paul, and it exists today.

What we are going to suggest is that many people are using the word *heretic* in ways that are not biblical and/or that do not align with its use in church tradition. And this, we believe, brings disrepute on the body of Christ.

Let's start by looking at the words *heresy* and *heretical* more closely and ask two key questions:

1. What does *heresy* mean in the New Testament?
2. What did *heresy* mean in early church history?

Heresy According to the New Testament Authors

Whenever we tell people how the New Testament authors understood the term *heresy*, they are shocked.

First, heresy wasn't the equivalent of false doctrine. Heresy was a specific practice, and a fleshly one at that.

According to Paul of Tarsus, to be a heretic meant that you formed a schism within a local body of believers. Thus, what qualified someone to be considered a heretic wasn't what they believed, but how they acted on their beliefs. If a person divided a genuine church, they were guilty of heresy.

Consequently, a person could be a heretic with the truth!

A Look at the Greek

According to *Vine's Expository Dictionary*, the Greek word *hairesis* denotes a choosing. The choice, says Vine, is an opinion that leads to a division or formation of a sect. "[It] properly denotes a predilection either for a particular truth or for a perversion of one," he notes, "generally with the expectation of personal advantage."

F. F. Bruce in his commentary on 1 Corinthians points out that *hairesis* in 1 Corinthians 11:19 and *schismata* in 1 Corinthians 11:18 are synonymous. Both words simply mean "divisions" or "factions." Thus a heretic is a person who causes divisions, dissensions, or factions.

If you think that dividing an authentic church isn't serious, think again. In 1 Corinthians 1:13a, Paul used the image of slicing Jesus Christ into pieces to depict how serious it is to divide an authentic church.

In Titus 3:10, Paul says to "warn a divisive person once, and then warn them a second time. After that, have nothing to do with them."

Paul uses the word *hairetikos* in this passage and it means "a heretic." But it doesn't refer to a person who holds wrong beliefs. According to BDAG (Bauer and Dank's Greek-English Lexicon), it "pertains to [one] causing divisions, factious, division-making, a division-maker."

As we should expect, modern versions of the Bible translate it as "anyone who causes divisions" (NRSV), "divisive man" (NKJV), "divisive person" (NIV), "factious man" (ASV, NASB), "person who stirs up division" (ESV), "someone who causes arguments" (NCV), and "troublemakers" (CEV). Not surprisingly, Paul lists *hairesis* (heresies or factions) as one of the works of the "flesh" (Galatians 5:19 NASB). A person who walks in the Spirit will always seek to build unity in the church. But a person who causes division walks in the flesh. Note that it's not the person's belief that is a "work of the flesh." It's their divisiveness.

As Ben Witherington notes in his social-rhetorical commentary on Galatians, *hairesis* (heresies) and *dichostasiai* (dissensions) in Galatians 5:20 both have in view those who "sever the body of Christ" and "use differences as an excuse to create factions."[1]

So, in the New Testament sense of the word, "heresy" was the creation of a division, a sect, a faction, or a party. For this reason, the author of Acts uses the word to describe the different sects within Judaism (Acts 5:17; 15:5; 24:5, 14; 26:5; 28:22).

Heresy involved the dividing of a local assembly, not the rightness or wrongness of what the dividing party believed.

It's true, of course, that a heresy could be created by someone pushing a false teaching on a local assembly, causing it to divide. Peter alludes to this when he warns that false teachers will secretly come into the church and introduce damnable *hairesis* (2 Peter 2:1 KJV).

To understand this verse, it's important to remember our earlier point that *hairesis* refers not to the rightness or wrongness of a belief, but to a choice that leads to a division or the formation of a sect.

This is what false teachers are going to introduce into the body of Christ, according to Peter, and they will divide the body. This is why he says they are "damnable." Again, division is a very serious thing to God.

In fact, this meaning is confirmed in the very next verse when Peter warns that many "will follow their depraved conduct and will bring the way of truth into disrepute" (v. 2).

If these false teachers had not introduced a choice into these congregations that led to divisions, they would still be false teachers, but they would not be heretics, according to the New Testament definition of the term.

In this light, we may say that a person who embraces a doctrine that we believe is false is misinformed (at best) or deceived (at worst). We may even consider them to be a potential heretic. But unless they use their belief to divide a body of believers by causing others to follow them and their false doctrine, they do not fit the biblical definition of a heretic.

So, if we wish to be biblical in our use of the word *heresy* or *heretical*, we should not refer to them as "heretics."

On the other hand, it's evident from the biblical understanding of heresy that a person could be a heretic who wasn't espousing a doctrine of any sort. Anyone who divides an authentic church for any reason would qualify as a heretic, according to the New Testament.

Peddling a Truth Heretically

As we mentioned earlier, a heretic could even be someone who espouses something good, but who does so in a divisive way.*

For example, suppose that a new church is planted. There is unity among the members. Their single focus is Jesus Christ. They are busy pursuing, knowing, loving, and serving Him together.

One day, Bob—a member of the church—announces, "I just discovered something I had never seen before. God really loves the poor. And He wants us to help the poor more than we already are." Serving the poor was one of the ways this congregation served their community, but Bob, with his newfound passion, wanted the church to be about little else.

Now, there's obviously nothing wrong with what Bob has said. And if Bob had submitted his insight to the community for prayerful discernment and given people time to grow into it, it might be that God could have used him to help this new congregation assign a higher priority to this ministry.

Unfortunately, this is not what Bob does. He grows frustrated that the community as a whole isn't catching his passion quick enough, so he begins to frequently invite to dinner the dozen or so in the church who seem more "on board" with his passion.

Caught in a snare of self-righteousness, he begins to use these times to sow seeds of judgment among his guests toward those in the congregation who "don't get it."

---

*For example, those who were creating division in the church in Corinth over their favorite apostle in 1 Corinthians 1 ("I'm of Paul," or "I'm of Apollos," or "I'm of Cephas" [v. 12 NKJV]) were acting heretically with something that was good and approved by God (viz. apostles). While Paul doesn't use the word "heresy" or "heretical" to describe these specific divisions, he does use the term *schismata* in 1 Corinthians 1:10, which carries the same essential meaning.

Before long, Bob announces that he and his recruits are leaving the church to start a new one that will reflect God's heart for the poor, according to Bob's standards. And he encourages others to join them.

Bob has just created a church split. He thus qualifies as a heretic in the New Testament sense of the word. Yet he is a heretic with the truth. Bob used a biblical truth in a fleshly way. He wielded it to create division among God's people.†

Heresy Later in Church History

Later in church history, most of the heretics—those who were dividing God's people—were peddling a false teaching. And so the word *heretic* came to be associated with false doctrine, very often doctrines that distorted the person of Jesus Christ.

But even in such cases, the label of *heresy* was applied to people who not only denied the foundational doctrines of orthodoxy but who actively worked against them.

Traditionally, the ecumenical creeds (Nicene, Apostles', Chalcedon) defined the parameters of orthodoxy, and therefore, they defined the parameters of heresy.

In this light, we submit that the word *heretic* should be applied only to people who work against the historic orthodox church as expressed by these creeds. Interestingly enough, however, these creeds say nothing about the many topics over which Christians today liberally drop the H-bomb on their fellow sisters and brothers in Christ.

---

†Keep in mind that we aren't saying that simply leaving a church (especially if it's truly a sect or is teaching false doctrine) is acting divisively. Nor is it divisive for a church to excommunicate someone based on unrepentant continued sin after many attempts have been made to urge them to repent (see Matthew 18). We aren't speaking about such situations.

The Key Takeaway

So what's our point?

Very simply, the way that countless Christians pull the lever of the H-bomb (heresy) on their fellow brethren today violates both the way the first-century Christians understood heresy as well as the later usage of the term in church history.

As we noted earlier, instead of reserving the word *heresy* for those who actively work against the church, and instead of accepting the ecumenical creeds as the ultimate criteria of orthodoxy, many today set up their own particular belief systems as the standard of "orthodoxy" and then drop the H-bomb on any who merely believe differently.

Sadly, most of those who are wrongly called heretics by some fellow Christians today are people who are completely orthodox according to the historic Christian creeds, and they are not dividing local assemblies. But some people have called them heretics simply because they hold to a particular view of Christ's coming, of ecclesiology, or of the gifts of the Spirit.

Others have been labeled heretics because they hold to a certain interpretation of Genesis 1, or to a particular understanding of God's sovereignty, or of election, free will, or the nature of the future.

So our argument really boils down to this:

If a person holds to beliefs that are in line with the historical Christian creeds (Nicene, Apostles', Chalcedon) and they are not dividing a local assembly of believers, then to call them a heretic is a gross and perverted use of the term.

And this kind of dubious branding grieves the Holy Spirit.

Our call, then, is for sisters and brothers in the body of Christ to align their use of the word *heretic* to the definitions of the New Testament and the early church. In so doing, we will see a whole lot less H-bomb dropping, and a whole lot less bloodletting in the body of Christ.

And that would give joy to the Holy Spirit!

25

They Are Our Teachers

To reiterate the point of this book in a slightly different way, if the major influencers of our faith retain our respect, but not our full agreement, should we not treat our fellow sisters and brothers in Christ as being in the transformational process rather than as finished products?

Or to put it another way, if we can include these figures in the kingdom despite some of their questionable views, why not include each other?

Note also that it can be argued, quite cogently I'd say, that many aberrant viewpoints are due to the exigencies of times and circumstances in which one lives.

This can be said about all the figures in church history whom I have covered. It also includes ourselves. I'm confident that if Calvin, Luther, Wesley, Edwards, Spurgeon, and the rest were living in our time, they'd find many views that Christians hold today to be "shocking."

On that point, I'd like to end this book by quoting the very people I've treated in this book on the importance of grace, humility, and the evils of divisiveness. In this way, they can serve as our teachers, even as they show us that God can use a person despite his or her "shocking beliefs."

C. S. Lewis

There are two kinds of love: we love wise and kind and beautiful people because we need them, but we love (or try to love) stupid and disagreeable people because they need us. This second kind is the more divine because that is how God loves us: not because we are lovable but because He is love, not because He needs to receive but He delights to give.[1]

Jonathan Edwards

A man of a right spirit is not a man of narrow and private views, but is greatly interested and concerned for the good of the community, to which he belongs, and particularly of the city or village in which he resides, and for the true welfare of the society of which he is a member.[2]

Martin Luther

I believe that there is upon earth a small holy flock, a holy assembly of pure saints under one head, Christ. They are called together by the Holy Spirit in one faith, one mind and one understanding. They possess many gifts, but are one in love and without sect or division.[3]

John Calvin

Does this not sufficiently indicate that a difference of opinion over these nonessential matters should in no wise be the basis of schism among Christians? First and foremost, we should agree on all points. But since all men are somewhat beclouded with ignorance, either we must leave no church remaining, or we must condone delusion in those matters which can go unknown without harm to the sum of religion and without loss of salvation.[4]

Augustine

In matters that are obscure and far beyond our vision, even in such as we may find treated in Holy Scripture, different Interpretations are sometimes possible without prejudice to the faith we have received. In such a case, we should not rush in headlong and so firmly take our stand on one side that, if further progress in the search of truth justly undermines this position, we too fall with it. That would be to battle not for the teaching of Holy Scripture but for our own, wishing its teaching to conform to ours, whereas we ought to wish ours to conform to that of Sacred Scripture.[5]

John Wesley

Beware you are not a fiery, persecuting enthusiast. Do not imagine that God has called you (just contrary to the spirit of Him you style your Master) to destroy men's lives, and not to save them. Never dream of forcing men into the ways of God. Think yourself, and let think. Use no constraint in matters of religion. Even those who are farthest out of the way never compel to come in by any other means than reason, truth, and love.[6]

Charles Spurgeon

Satan always hates Christian fellowship; it is his policy to keep Christians apart. Anything that can divide saints from one another he delights in. He attaches far more importance to godly intercourse than we do. Since union is strength, he does his best to promote separation.[7]

D. L. Moody

I have never yet known the Spirit of God to work where the Lord's people were divided.[8]

Billy Graham

[Jesus] prayed for unity among believers. God, who wills man's unity in Christ, is a God of variety. So often we want everyone to be the same—to think and speak and believe as we do. Many Scripture passages could be called to witness that love is the real key to Christian unity. In the spirit of true humility, compassion, consideration, and unselfishness, we are to approach our problems, our work, and even our differences.[9]

Acknowledgments

To Rick Warren, for signing my death warrant by asking me to create the original blog series which formed the basis for this book. To James Swan of *Beggars All: Reformation and Apologetics* for checking every source with his razor-sharp eye for detail, for adding additional historical information, and for his helpful editorial work. To Tonya Ragan, Jared Stump, Jaime O'Donnell, William Hemsworth, and Isabella Bosch for assisting me with some of the sources. (If you find any flaws in the documentation, it's my fault, not theirs!) To Thomas Schmidt for his helpful feedback on the manuscript. To the Baker team, for getting out on a limb (and sawing hard) in order to put this book into the world.

Notes

A Word to Scholars

This book wasn't written to or for scholars. It was written for the masses. However, I have provided the following sources to show readers that the "shocking beliefs" I've listed in each chapter weren't invented out of whole cloth.

Some of the sources I provide are firsthand materials. Others are secondhand sources taken from historians who drew from firsthand documents.

Some scholars may quibble with certain historians (like Will Durant). But Durant and the other historians I've cited have not been debunked in the specific points where I cite them. Therefore, if you have a quibble with a "shocking belief" that I've listed in this book, write me directly and show me exactly where and how my information is incorrect.

If you are right, the information will be corrected in a future reprint. If you cannot, however, please don't blow bubbles by criticizing the work for using secondhand sources or citing historians whom you don't respect. Be a little taller than that, would you?

You can find my email address on the contact page of my blog—frankviola.org.

That said (yes, I'll repeat it one more time), the point of the book isn't found in a specific "shocking belief" held by one of the great Christians of the past. The point is that each figure in church history held to flawed ideas, so let's be more gracious in our theological dialogue today.

Chapter 3 We Know in Part

1. Frank Viola, *Revise Us Again* (Colorado Springs: David C. Cook, 2010).

Chapter 4 Honoring Those with Whom You Disagree

1. John Whitehead, *The Life of the Rev. John Wesley, M.A., with the Life of the Rev. Charles Wesley, M.A.* (London: John E. Beardsley, 1793), 529.

2. Warren W. Wiersbe, *Wycliffe Handbook of Preaching and Preachers* (Chicago: Moody, 1984), 255.

Chapter 5 It's Not a Bloodsport

1. If you'd like to read the details on this "trail of blood," the following books recount the tragic story: E. H. Broadbent, *The Pilgrim Church* (Grand Rapids: Gospel Folio Press, 1999); Kim Tan, *Lost Heritage* (Surrey, England: Highland Books, 1996); and Leonard Verduin, *The Reformers and Their Stepchildren* (Grand Rapids: Eerdmans, 1964).

Chapter 6 The Shocking Beliefs of C. S. Lewis

1. Philip Ryken, "Lewis as the Patron Saint of American Evangelicalism," in Judith Wolfe and B. N. Wolfe, eds., *C. S. Lewis and the Church: Essays in Honour of Walter Hooper* (New York: T&T Clark International, 2011), 174–85.

2. J. I. Packer, "Still Surprised by Lewis," *Christianity Today*, September 7, 1998, 55.

3. "Religion: Don v. Devil," *Time*, September 8, 1947.

4. Packer, "Still Surprised by Lewis," 60.

5. Peter Kreeft, *Between Heaven and Hell* (Downers Grove, IL: InterVarsity, 1982). Interestingly, Aldous Huxley died on the same day also. Kreeft presents a fictional dialogue between Lewis, Kennedy, and Huxley in the afterlife. Strikingly, both Lewis and Kennedy were called "Jack" by their friends. But that's neither here nor there.

6. Joel S. Woodruff, "The Generous Heart and Life of C. S. Lewis," *Knowing and Doing*, September 2013; John Blake, "The C. S. Lewis You Never Knew," CNN Belief (blog), December 1, 2013.

7. Blake, "C. S. Lewis You Never Knew"; Alister McGrath, *C. S. Lewis, A Life: Eccentric Genius, Reluctant Prophet* (Carol Stream, IL: Tyndale, 2013), 166.

8. Blake, "C. S. Lewis You Never Knew"; McGrath, *C. S. Lewis, A Life*, 163.

9. Joel S. Woodruff, "C. S. Lewis's Humble and Thoughtful Gift of Letter Writing," *Knowing and Doing*, Fall 2013.

10. Blake, "C. S. Lewis You Never Knew"; McGrath, *C. S. Lewis, A Life*, 67–69.

11. Blake, "C. S. Lewis You Never Knew."

12. Blake, "C. S. Lewis You Never Knew." Lewis's wife (Joy Davidman) was an American poet and writer who was seventeen years younger than Lewis. Note that Lewis wrote much after *Grief*, and several biographers recount that Lewis felt he lost a debate to an Oxford professor, pre Joy's death, and this is what provoked him to modify his approach.

13. C. S. Lewis, *Letters to Malcolm* (San Francisco: HarperOne, 2017), 144.

14. Lewis, *Letters to Malcolm*, 145–46. Note that Lewis distanced himself from "the romish doctrine concerning Purgatory," but he positively referred to the Roman Catholic convert John Henry Newman's *Dream of Gerontius* as expressing the "right view." Lewis appeared to believe there was a kind of *golden age* orthodox Christian view of purgatory, which became corrupted, and then was reclaimed by Cardinal Newman.

15. Lewis, *Letters to Malcolm*, 145.

16. C. S. Lewis, *Mere Christianity* (New York: Collier Books, 1960), 176–77. Lewis wrote,

> In the first place the situation in the actual world is much more complicated than that. The world does not consist of 100 per cent. Christians and 100 per cent. Non-Christians. There are people (a great many of them) who are slowly ceasing to be Christians but who still call themselves by that name: some of them are clergymen. There are other people who are slowly becoming Christians though they do not yet call themselves so. There are people who do not accept the full Christian doctrine about Christ but who are so strongly attracted by Him that they are His in a much deeper sense than they themselves understand. There are people in other religions who are being led by God's secret influence to concentrate on those parts of their religion which are in agreement with Christianity, and who thus belong to Christ without knowing it. (Lewis, *Mere Christianity*, 209–10)

He also said,

> Of course it should be pointed out that, though all salvation is through Jesus, we need not conclude that He cannot save those who have not explicitly accepted Him in this life. (C. S. Lewis, *God in the Dock* [Grand Rapids: William B. Eerdmans, 1970], 101–2)

17. Lewis explained this belief in a letter to Audrey Sutherland dated April 28, 1960. See *Collected Letters*, vol. 3, 1147–48.

See also C. S. Lewis, *The Great Divorce* (New York: Macmillan, 1946), 126–30; and C. S. Lewis, *The Last Battle* (New York: Macmillan, 1956), 150–57. In the latter work, we encounter in heaven a Calormene (Muslim) who is surprised to be there. Aslan says to the Calormene, "Beloved, said the Glorious one, unless thy desire had been for me thou wouldst not have sought so long and so truly. For all will find what they truly seek" (p. 156). It is important to note that Lewis was always tentative about such speculative matters. He was attracted to, though not quite persuaded by, his spiritual mentor George MacDonald's notion that God will use even hell to turn people to Himself. But Lewis's strong belief in free will led him to the conclusion that we get what we want, and some want hell. Finally, almost all of the souls in hell in *The Great Divorce* choose to remain where they are. According to Lewis, people continue to make decisions after death. *The Last Battle* seems to imply that this number doesn't include everyone who has not heard the gospel, but only for those who were already making fundamental choices in life that were moving toward Christ.

18. C. S. Lewis, *George MacDonald, An Anthology* (New York: Macmillan, 1978), xxx–xxxi. Lewis was only seven years old when MacDonald died. Lewis said of him, "All that I know of George MacDonald I have learned either from his own books or from the biography which his son, Dr. Greenville MacDonald, published in 1924; nor have I ever, but once, talked of him to anyone who had met him" (Lewis, *George MacDonald*, xxi).

19. Lewis, *Mere Christianity*, 78.

20. C. S. Lewis, *Reflections on the Psalms* (San Francisco: HarperCollins, 2017), 128.

21. Lewis, *Reflections on the Psalms*, 130. Lewis expands his thoughts on this topic on pages 130 and following.

22. Lewis, *Reflections on the Psalms*, 22. On page 130, Lewis expands his thoughts on this remark.

23. Lewis, *Reflections on the Psalms*, 128.

24. J. I. Packer in "Still Surprised by Lewis," *Christianity Today*, September 7, 1998, 56.

25. Packer, "Still Surprised by Lewis," 60.

Chapter 7 The Shocking Beliefs of Jonathan Edwards

1. Walter A. Elwell, *Evangelical Dictionary of Theology* (Grand Rapids: Baker Academic, 2001), 366.

2. Robert W. Jensen, *America's Theologian: A Recommendation of Jonathan Edwards* (New York: Oxford University Press, 1992). Some historians haven't been shy about opining that Edwards was America's greatest intellectual and theologian, or words to that effect.

3. Jonathan Edwards, "Letter to the Reverend John Erskine, Northampton, July 5, 1750," in *Letters and Personal Writings*, The Works of Jonathan Edwards (*WJE*) 16:355; *WJE*, vol. 1 (London: Ball, Arnold, and Co., 1840), clxiii. See also Jonathan Gibson, "Jonathan Edwards: A Missionary?" published on the *themelios* website.

4. Michael Bird, "If John Edwards Was Here Today!" Patheos, August 10, 2012; see also Gerald R McDermott, "Jonathan Edwards and American Indians: The Devil Sucks Their Blood," *New England Quarterly*, December 1999; 72, 4;

ProQuest Direct Complete p. 539. The article explains Edwards's defense of the Native Americans along with his changing attitude toward them. It's an example of a man coming out of a racial attitude and experiencing a kind of social redemption.

5. Edwards usually spoke quietly and without exaggerated gestures. "He never used loud volume or exaggerated gestures to make his points, for he relied on striking imagery and the logical argument of his sermons" (*Christian History* 4, no. 4 [1985]: 6).

6. For a detailed examination of Edwards and slavery, see Sherard Burns, "Trusting the Theology of a Slave Owner," in John Piper and Justin Taylor, eds., *A God-Entranced Vision of All Things: The Legacy of Jonathan Edwards* (Wheaton: Crossway, 2004), 145–74; George Mardson, *Jonathan Edwards: A Life* (New Haven: Yale University Press, 2004), 255–58; and Kenneth P. Minkema, "Jonathan Edwards's Defense of Slavery," *Massachusetts Historical Review* 4 (2002): 23–59.

7. Thabiti Anyabwile, "Jonathan Edwards, Slavery, and the Theology of African Americans," paper presented at Trinity Evangelical Divinity School, February 1, 2012.

8. Robert C. Fuller, *Naming the Antichrist: The History of an American Obsession* (New York: Oxford University Press, 1995), 66. See also Glen R. Kreider, *Jonathan Edwards's Interpretation of Revelation 4:1–8:1* (New York: University Press of America, 2004), 157; and Christopher B. Holdsworth, "The Eschatology of Jonathan Edwards," *Reformation and Revival* 5, no. 3 (Summer 1996).

9. Jonathan Edwards, *The Works of President Edwards*, vol. 4 (New York: Leavitt & Allen, 1852), 318.

10. Note that Edwards explains in the sermon that the imagery of the subject was intended for "awakening unconverted persons in this congregation." Edwards wasn't simply ranting about God's hatred of sinners. The entire sermon was a form of evangelism. His goal was to provoke the sinner to trust in Christ and be saved. For a good overview, see John Gerstner, "Justifying a Scare Theology," in *Jonathan Edwards, Evangelist* (Morgan, PA: Soli Deo Gloria Publications, 1995), 24–33.

11. Jonathan Edwards, *The Works of President Edwards*, vol. 3 (New York: Leavitt & Allen, 1858), 313.

12. It should be noted that one author nuances the point. He writes,

At no time did Edwards believe or preach that America would be either the focus or the locus of the coming millennium. Rather, he suggested that, at best, America may be where those intermittent revivals would occur that eventually would bring on the millennium, the latter being at least 250 years away. . . . Much of the confusion concerning Edwards' beliefs came from one statement in his *Some Thoughts Concerning the Revival* (1742) where he declared that "this work of God's Spirit [i.e., the revival, the Great Awakening], that is so extraordinarily and wonderful, is the dawning, or at least a prelude, of that glorious work of God, so often foretold in Scripture. He later said that this "glorious work of God . . . must be near." (C. Samuel Storms, *Signs of the Spirit: An Interpretation of Jonathan Edwards' Religious Affections* [Wheaton: Crossway, 2007],186–88)

But "that glorious work of God" was not a reference to the millennium itself but "to a long period of intermittent revival that would lead up to the millennium"

(Sam Storms, "The Eschatology of Jonathan Edwards," SamStorms.com, posted on May 2, 2009). That said, Edwards did write, "And there are many things that make it probable that this work will begin in America" (Edwards, *Works of President Edwards*, 3:313).

13. Much of this can be found in two of Edwards's books, *Distinguishing Marks of a Work of the Spirit of God* and *A Faithful Narrative of the Surprising Work of God*. Both books detail Edwards's theology on the supernatural and support the statements I've made regarding emotional outbursts. Excerpts can be found at radicalresurgence.com/edwards.

14. See Phil Roberts, *Lessons from the Past—The Discernment of Signs: Jonathan Edwards and the Toronto Blessing*, paper presented to the Evangelical Theological Society in Philadelphia, November 17, 1995.

15. Henry Sheldon, *History of the Christian Church*, vol. 4 (New York: Thomas Y. Crowell, 1895), 245.

16. The rest of the quote is as follows:

> I have *many times* had *a sense of the glory* of the third person in the Trinity, in his office of Sanctifier; in his holy operations, communicating divine light and life to the soul. God, in the communications of his Holy Spirit, has *appeared* as an infinite fountain of divine glory and sweetness; being full, and sufficient to fill and satisfy the soul; pouring forth itself in sweet communications; like the sun in its glory, sweetly and pleasantly diffusing light and life. And I have sometimes had *an affecting sense* of the excellency of the word of God, as a word of life; as the light of life; a sweet, excellent life-giving word; accompanied with a thirsting after that word, that it might dwell richly in my heart. (Jonathan Edwards, *The Works of President Edwards*, vol. 1 [New York: Leavitt & Allen, 1843], 25, emphasis mine)

17. Roger Olson, "Why Is Jonathan Edwards Considered So Great?" *Patheos*, July 31, 2012. For details on this point and other objections Olson has with Edwards's theology, see Roger Olson, *The Story of Christian Theology* (Downers Grove, IL: IVP Academic, 1999), 504–19.

18. Olson, *Story of Christian Theology*, 512.

Chapter 8 The Shocking Beliefs of Martin Luther

1. Stephen E. Whicher and Robert E. Spiller, *The Early Lectures of Ralph Waldo Emerson*, vol. 1 (Cambridge, MA: Belknap Press, 1966), 119.

2. *Christian History* 11, no. 2: 15. In *Luther's Works* (LW) (Philadelphia: Fortress; St. Louis: Concordia, 1958–86, 2008–), 34:336–37, the great Reformer stated that he "meditated day and night" on the righteousness of God. So the revelation didn't appear to come to him all at once.

3. Erwin Iserloh, *The Theses Were Not Posted: Luther between Reform and Reformation* (Boston: Beacon Press, 1968); Kurt Aland, *Martin Luther's 95 Theses, with the Pertinent Documents of the History of the Reformation*, trans. P. J. Schroeder et al. (St. Louis: Concordia, 1967); and "Martin Luther's 95 Theses Are 500 Years Old. Here's Why They're Still Causing Controversy," *Time*, October 31, 2017.

4. *LW*, 54:311.

5. Gotthelf Wiedermann, "Cochlaeus as Polemicist," found in Peter Newman Brooks, ed., *Seven-Headed Luther* (Oxford: Clarendon Press, 1983), 198; *Christian History* 11, no. 2: 28.

6. *Christian History* 11, no. 2: 28; Roland Bainton, *Here I Stand: A Life of Martin Luther* (New York: Abingdon-Cokesbury Press, 1950), 296.

7. Cited by Bainton in *Here I Stand*, 298, as well as Preserved Smith, *The Life and Letters of Martin Luther* (London: Forgotten Books, 2012), 284; *Christian History* 12, no. 3: 3.

8. For an interesting new biography on Luther, see Brad S. Gregory, *Rebel in the Ranks* (New York: HarperOne, 2017).

9. *LW*, 45:229.

10. The reason is because he had had some negative interactions with the Jews over the interpretation of Scripture. He also became convinced they were proselytizing Christians to convert to Judaism.

11. This remark was part of a rhetorical argument in which Luther accepted the negative Jewish stereotypes of his day. Luther, in responding to what he believed the Jews were saying and doing to Christians (kidnapping and killing Christian children), says, "We lodge them, we let them eat and drink with us. We do not kidnap their children and pierce them through." Luther then argues,

> So we are even at fault in not avenging all this innocent blood of our Lord and of the Christians which they shed for three hundred years after the destruction of Jerusalem, and the blood of the children they have shed since then (which still shines forth from their eyes and their skin). We are at fault in not slaying them. Rather we allow them to live freely in our midst despite all their murdering, cursing, blaspheming, lying, and defaming; we protect and shield their synagogues, houses, life, and property. In this way we make them lazy and secure and encourage them to fleece us boldly of our money and goods, as well as to mock and deride us, with a view to finally overcoming us, killing us all for such a great sin, and robbing us of all our property (as they daily pray and hope). Now tell me whether they do not have every reason to be the enemies of us accursed Goyim, to curse us and to strive for our final, complete, and eternal ruin! (*LW*, 47:267)

12. Bainton, *Here I Stand*, 379.

13. *LW*, 47:269ff.

14. Quoted in Kirsi Stjerna and Brooks Schramm, *Martin Luther, the Bible, and the Jewish People: A Reader* (Minneapolis: Fortress Press, 2012), 179. The primary source is the Weimar edition of Luther's works, also known as the Weimarer Ausgabe (WA) (Germany: Weimar, 1883–2009), 53:580.

15. James Swan points out,

> In Luther studies there have been a number of researchers who conclude Luther's later anti-Jewish tracts were written from a position different than current anti-semitism. Luther was born into a society that was anti-Judaic, but it was not the current anti-Judaic type of society that bases its racism on biological factors. Luther had no objections to integrating converted Jews into Christian society. He had nothing against Jews as "Jews." He had something against their religion because he believed it denied and

blasphemed Christ. If one frames the issues with these two categories (anti-semitism, anti-Judaic), Luther was not anti-semitic. The contemporary use of the word "anti-semitism" though does not typically consider its distinction from anti-Judaism. The word now has a more broad meaning including anti-Judaism. The current debate centers around whether the evolved use of the term is a significant step towards describing previous history or if it's setting up an anachronistic standard for evaluating previous history. As I've looked at this issue from time to time, I'm beginning to think more along the lines of evaluating Luther with the current understanding of the word anti-semitism. (Luther, WA, 53:502, quoted in James Swan, "Luther: The Jews Deserve to Be Hanged on Gallows Seven Times Higher Than Ordinary Thieves," *Beggars All: Reformation & Apologetics* [blog], Dec. 8, 2016, http://beggarsallreformation.blogspot.com/2016/12/luther-jews-deserve-to-be-hanged-on.html)

16. *LW*, 45:25.

17. Cited in James Swan, "Martin Luther's Attitude toward the Jews," Internet Archive, June 2005, sec. 3.

18. *LW*, 45:33.

19. *LW*, 36:105.

20. Quoted in M. Audin, *History of the Life, Writings, and Doctrines of Luther*, vol. 2 (London: C. Dolman, 1854), 184. Note that Luther's final position on polygamy was, "Anyone who . . . takes more than one wife, and thinks that this is right, the devil will prepare for him a bath in the depths of hell. Amen." WA, 53:195–96.

21. Luther's opinion on the book of Revelation changed and his views on Hebrews fluctuated.

22. *LW*, 35:362. Swan notes that Luther later deleted this paragraph. It no longer appears in editions after 1522. (See James Swan, "Luther's 'Epistle of Straw' Comment," *Beggars All: Reformation & Apologetics* [blog], June 20, 2008). John Warwick Montgomery points out: "Few people realize—and liberal Luther interpreters do not particularly advertise the fact—that in all the editions of Luther's Bible translation after 1522 the Reformer dropped the paragraphs at the end, of his general Preface to the New Testament which made value judgments among the various biblical books and which included the famous reference to James as an 'Epistle of straw.'" John Warwick Montgomery, "Lessons from Luther on the Inerrancy of Holy Writs," *Westminster Theological Journal* 36: 295.

23. *LW*, 35:395–96.

24. *LW*, 46:50. See also *LW*, 46:54, 65–66, for more alarming quotes on this topic.

25. Herbert Albert Laurens Fisher, *A History of Europe*, vol. 2 (London: Eyre and Spottiswoode, 1935), 506. Durant includes more shocking quotes from Luther on the peasants' revolt. See Will Durant, *The Reformation* (New York: Simon & Schuster, 1957), 389–95.

26. Martin Luther, *Luther's Correspondence and Other Contemporary Letters*, trans. and ed. Preserved Smith, vol. 2 (Lutheran Publication Society, 1918; repr., Ithica, NY: Cornell University Library, 2012), 321.

27. *LW*, 54:180. Note that this is a comment from Table Talk, thus something Luther is purported to have said. It is not something he wrote.

28. Bainton, *Here I Stand*, 376.

29. Roland H. Bainton, *The Travel of Religious Liberty* (Eugene, OR: Wipft & Stock, 1951), 64. See also Peter Hoover, *Secret of the Strength* (Shippensburg, PA: Benchmark Press, 1999), 59, 198. It should be noted that Luther changed his position on the death penalty for Anabaptists later in his life. His position evolved to where only seditious Anabaptists were to be executed. For details, see James Swan, "Here I Stand: A Review of Dave Armstrong's Citations of Roland Bainton's Popular Biography on Martin Luther," Internet Archive, July 2004.

30. Mark U. Edwards Jr., *Luther's Last Battles: Politics and Polemics 1531–46* (London: Cornell University Press, 1983), 6. The primary source for both quotes are Table Talk utterance, Trischreden (WA TR), 2:455 (no. 2410a) and *D. Martin Luthers Werke* (WA) (Weimer: Böhlau, 1883–1993), 30.2:68, *LW*, 59:250, respectively.

31. Ewald Plass, *What Luther Says: An Anthology*, vol. 2 (St. Louis: Concordia Publishing House, 1959), 1058. Plass took this quote from Briefswechsel [Correspondence] (WA BR) 2:44f.

32. *LW*, 41:308.

33. WA, 53:580. Luther refers to "Judas Piss" on page 636. See also *Christian History* 12, no. 3: 35.

34. *LW*, 39:207; Plass, *What Luther Says*, 2:1059. The "goat" was a reference to Jerome Emser.

35. *Masterpieces of Eloquence: Famous Orations of Great World Leaders from Early Greece to the Present Time*, vol. 4 (New York: P. F. Collier & Son, 1905), 1336–37.

36. Quoted in Harry Gerald Haile, *Luther: An Experiment in Biography* (New Jersey: Princeton University Press, 1980), 119.

37. *Christian History* 12, no. 3: 37.

38. Roland Bainton put it this way: "The volume of coarseness, in his total output is slight. Detractors have sifted from the pitchblende of his ninety tomes a few pages of radioactive vulgarity." Bainton, *Here I Stand*, 232.

39. *Christian History* 12, no. 3: 20–21.

40. *Christian History* 12, no. 3: 41.

41. *LW*, 54:73.

42. *Christian History* 12, no. 3: 43.

43. *LW*, 54:48.

44. Luther, "Concerning the Ministry," *LW*, 40:35.

45. John Milton, *The Poetical Works of John Milton* (London: Edward Churton, 1838), 453.

46. Emil Brunner, *The Misunderstanding of the Church* (London: Lutterworth Press, 1952), 15–16.

Chapter 9 The Shocking Beliefs of John Calvin

1. *The Autobiography of Charles H. Spurgeon*, vol. 2 (Chicago: Fleming H. Revell Company, 1899), 372. The second Spurgeon quote is often attributed to a

footnote in Ian Murray's book *The Forgotten Spurgeon* (Morgan, PA: The Banner of Truth Trust, 1998), 79. Murray says the quote is from G. Holden Pike's biography of Spurgeon, *The Life and Work of Charles Haddon Spurgeon*, vol. 6, p. 197. It appears to be a recorded statement that Spurgeon made at "the annual college picnic," not something he actually wrote. An extended version of the quote appears as follows: "The longer he lived," said Mr. Spurgeon, "the clearer did it appear that John Calvin's system was the—nearest to perfection; for, if all other divines stood on each other's shoulders they would not reach up to the reformer's toes." *Dublin University Magazine* 90, July–Dec. 1877, 634.

2. Philip Schaff, *History of the Christian Church*, vol. 7 (New York: Charles Scribner's Sons, 1907), 834.

3. Schaff, *History of the Christian Church*, 7:277. Schaff's quote of Voltaire is a truncated version. Voltaire actually said,

This religion of Geneva was not absolutely the same as that of the Swiss: but the difference is inconsiderable; and it never altered their communion. The famous Calvin, whom we look upon as the apostle of Geneva, had no share in this change: he retired some time after to this town; but was soon expelled, his doctrine not being in every respect conformable to the established religion; he came back again, and became Pope of the Protestant party. (Voltaire, *The Universal History & State of Europe*, vol. 2 [Edinburgh: Sands, Donaldson, Murray & Cochran, 1758], 240)

4. Will Durant, *The Reformation: The Story of Civilization* (New York: Simon and Schuster, 1957), 472.

5. For a helpful overview of the multitude of theological errors of Servetus, see Schaff, *History of the Christian Church*, 736–57.

6. Servetus wasn't just condemned by Calvin. He was universally condemned as a heretic according to the basic Western worldview of the sixteenth century. The Roman Catholic Church had previously captured and condemned Servetus; he received a death sentence, but then managed to escape. This, of course, was before he was eventually burned to death in Geneva.

7. Jules Bonnet, *Letters of John Calvin: Compiled from the Original Manuscripts and Edited with Historical Notes*, vol. 2 (Edinburgh: Thomas Constable and Co., 1857), 19. Some have argued that statements like this were hyperbolic, not literal, on Calvin's part. But the historical facts comport with the overall point that Calvin did approve of Servetus's death. For two solid biographies of Calvin, see Alister McGrath, *A Life of John Calvin* (New Jersey: Wiley-Blackwell, 1993) and Gordon F. Bruce, *Calvin* (New Haven: Yale University Press, 2009).

8. This quote is from a letter Calvin wrote to William Farel, August 20, 1553. Lorraine Boettner, *The Reformed Doctrine of Predestination* (New Jersey: Presbyterian and Reformed Publishing Company, 1932), 417; Bonnet's translation of the letter reads, "I hope that sentence of death will at least be passed upon him; but I desire that the severity of the punishment may be mitigated." Jules Bonnet, *Letters of John Calvin*, vol. 2 (Edinburgh: Thomas Constable and Co., 1 857), 399.

9. Quoted in Schaff, *History of the Christian Church*, 690–91.

10. Schaff, *History of the Christian Church*, 791.

11. Perez Zagorin, *How the Idea of Religious Toleration Came to the West* (New Jersey: Princeton University Press, 2003), 116.

12. Durant, *Reformation*, 486.

13. This brings up another point. Consider for a moment if execution for heresy was legal in our time. If it were, I think we'd have a lot of dead Christians who lost their lives at the hands of other Christians over doctrinal trespasses. If you think I'm wrong, just watch the vitriol and hatred in many "Christian" online forums as they verbally bludgeon one another over theological interpretations.

14. John Calvin, *Institutes of the Christian Religion* (Philadelphia: The Westminster Press, 1960), 4.17.32. Calvin wrote, "If anyone should ask me how this takes place, I shall not be ashamed to confess that it is a secret too lofty for either my mind to comprehend or my words to declare." 4.17.31–32. For Calvin the Lord's Supper was a means of feeling a sense of assurance that Christ died for us and that we are now risen with Him, and will rise with Him in the future "immortality of our flesh."

15. William Manchester, *A World Lit Only by Fire* (New York: Sterling, 2014), 190. Keep in mind that sixteenth-century polemicists routinely treated their opponents contemptuously as the common method of debate and disagreement. Luther felt his harsh language was simply following the example of Christ. Luther asked rhetorically if the Lord used abusive language against his enemies, saying: "Was he abusive when he called the Jews an adulterous and perverse generation, an offspring of vipers, hypocrites, and children of the Devil? . . . The truth, which one is conscious of possessing, cannot be patient against its obstinate and intractable enemies." Martin Luther, cited by Eric Gritsch, "The Unrefined Reformer," *Christian History* 12, no. 3: 36.

16. *The Mennonite Encyclopedia* comments, "Calvin's judgment of Menno Simons is incomprehensible; he knew him, to be sure, only through a letter from Martin Micron. In an opinion sent to Micron he said, 'Nothing can be prouder, nothing more impudent than this donkey (Calv. IV, 176; *HRE* XII, 592).'" Cornelius J. Dyck and Dennis D. Martin, *The Mennonite Encyclopedia*, vol. 1 (Mennonite Brethren Publishing House, 1955), 497.

17. Durant, *Reformation*, 473. For information on Calvin's role in Geneva, see Robert M. Kingdon, *Registers of the Consistory of Geneva in the Time of Calvin*, vol. 1 (Grand Rapids: Eerdmans, 1996). This latter book contains a record of the Genevan Consistory, and how Calvin's voice and will functioned during the proceedings.

18. Historians disagree over how much influence Calvin had in Geneva. Some believe he had enormous influence on everything that went on in the city from 1542 until his death. One historian put it this way:

> To get a glimpse of Calvin's influence on political thinking in his own day, we must turn first of all to the city of Geneva, in which he lived. He undoubtedly wielded considerable influence on the codification of Geneva's laws, as he was the secretary of the committee appointed to put the laws into a proper form. During the years following 1542, when the laws were codified, he also exerted no little personal influence on the governing bodies of the city. (*Christian History* 4, no. 4: 30)

Others believe he didn't have great influence there. According to one source, [Calvin] had become close friends with leading Reformers like Martin Bucer and Philip Melanchthon. He was asked to return to Geneva by city authorities, and he spent the rest of his life trying to help establish a theocratic society. . . .

He was in no way the ruler or dictator of Geneva. He was appointed by the city council and paid by them. He could at any time have been dismissed by them (as he had been in 1538). He was a foreigner in Geneva, not even a naturalized citizen, until near the end of his life. His was a moral authority, stemming from his belief that, because he proclaimed the message of the Bible, he was God's ambassador, with divine authority behind him. As such, he was involved in much that went on in Geneva, from the city constitution to drains and heating appliances." (Quoted in "John Calvin, Father of the Reformed Faith," *Christian History* at ChristianityToday.com, https://www.christianitytoday.com/history/people/theologians/john-calvin.html)

See also Alister E. McGrath, *A Life of John Calvin: A Study in the Shaping of Western Culture* (West Sussex, UK: Wiley-Blackwell, 1993), 109. Either way, Calvin had influence in Geneva. That doesn't mean that everything that happened there can be laid at his feet. Nor does it mean that he had no role to play at all.

19. James Harvey Robinson, *Readings in European History*, vol. 2 (Boston: Ginn, 1906), 134.

20. Durant, *Reformation*, 473.

21. Durant, *Reformation*.

22. Durant, *Reformation*.

23. Durant, *Reformation*, 474.

24. Durant, *Reformation*.

25. Durant, *Reformation*.

26. Durant, *Reformation*.

27. Durant, *Reformation*. Note that "Claude" refers to Saint Claude. There was a Shrine to this saint in the area. The authorities had this name-rule to usher in the complete rejection of Romanism and promote Reformation.

28. Durant, *Reformation*.

29. Charles Beard, *The Reformation of the Sixteenth Century*, 2nd ed. (London: Williams and Norgate, 1885), 250.

30. Durant, *Reformation*.

31. Durant, *Reformation*.

32. Durant, *Reformation*.

33. Durant, *Reformation*, 476. Some sources say it was "two of Calvin's own female relatives." Preserved Smith, *The Age of Reformation* (New York: Henry Holt and Company, 1920), 173–74. Another source says, "In 1562, his step-daughter, Judith, fell into similar disgrace—a matter which Calvin felt so keenly that he left the city to seek the solitude of the country for a few days after the misdeed became public knowledge." Williston Walker, *John Calvin* (New York: G. P. Putnam's Sons, 1906), 358. And another states,

Although Calvin was thus ceaselessly busy in supervising the morals of the citizens of Geneva, he found to his chagrin that neither his example nor his vigilance could secure the good behaviour of his own household. Antoine Calvin and his wife lived in the same house with the Reformer, and Antoine's wife was unsatisfactory. The charge of immoral conduct which was brought against her in 1548 was dismissed as not proven, but in January, 1557, she was caught in the act of adultery with Calvin's hunchback servant, Pierre Daguet, under Calvin's own roof. On the 14th Calvin appeared before the Consistory on behalf of his brother and asked for divorce. The court was slow to move, and on 6 February Calvin wrote to Farel: "We are almost overwhelmed by domestic troubles. The judges do not see a reason for releasing my brother. I think their blindness is a just punishment for ours, for during two whole years I was being robbed by that thief and I saw nothing. But if judgment is not given soon, we mean to bring the matter to an issue in another way." (Hugh Young Reyburn, *John Calvin* [New York: Hodder and Stroughton, 1914], 210)

34. Durant, *Reformation*, 473.

35. Durant, *Reformation*, 476. That there was a "high percentage" of these events is disputed by some.

36. John Hubbird, "Calvin's Geneva—An Experiment in Christian Theocracy" at radicalresurgence.com/calvinsgeneva. See also Harro Hopfl, *The Church Polity of John Calvin* (New York: Cambridge University Press, 1985), 136. For more information on Calvin's Geneva, see Obie Ephyhm, "Calvin's Geneva—Applied Critical Thinking" at radicalresurgence.com/calvinsgenevaapplied.

37. John Calvin, *Commentaries on the Book of the Prophet Daniel*, vol. 1 (Edinburgh: Calvin Translation Society, 1852), 185. Some believe that Calvin was speaking about Jewish biblical interpretation rather than an all-out inclusive remark about all Jews. You can make up your own mind.

38. Jeremy Cohen, ed., *Essential Papers on Judaism and Christianity in Conflict, From Late Antiquity to the Reformation* (New York: New York University Press, 1991), 381. The chapter is by Salo W. Baron, "John Calvin and the Jews," 380–400.

39. John Calvin, *Institutes of the Christian Religion*, 3.21.5; vol. 2 (Edinburgh: T&T Clark, 1863), 206. The Battles translation states it a bit differently: "For all are not created in equal condition; rather, eternal life is foreordained for some, eternal damnation for others. Therefore, as any man has been created to one or the other of these ends, we speak of him as predestined to life or to death." It should be noted that some Calvinists reject the type of double predestination in which God deliberately creates a person for damnation apart from the fall of humanity. In a similar way, there is also debate within Reformed theology as to whether or not Calvin was an infralapsarian or a supralapsarian.

40. Calvin, *Institutes of Christian Religion*, 3.23.5.

Chapter 10 The Shocking Beliefs of Augustine

1. Richard N. Ostling, "The Second Founder of Our Faith," *Time*, Sept. 29, 1986. The author of the article states, "Only a handful of thinkers have had equivalent influence over such a span of years. Yale historian Jaroslav Pelikan observes . . . that in each of the sixteen centuries since his conversion, Augustine has been a 'major intellectual, spiritual and cultural force.'" *Time* magazine took

this quote from Jaroslav Pelikan, *The Mystery of Continuity: Time and History, Memory and Eternity in the Thought of Saint Augustine* (Charlottesville: University Press of Virginia, 1986), 140. Pelikan says, "There has, quite literally, been no century of the sixteen centuries since the conversion of Augustine in which he has not been a major intellectual, spiritual, and cultural force." See also *Christian History* 6, no. 3: 2.

2. B. B. Warfield, "Augustine and His 'Confessions,'" *Princeton Theological Review,* vol. 3 (Philadelphia: MacCalla & Co. Inc., 1905), 124, 126. Warfield writes, "It was equally he who by his doctrine of grace contributed the factor of positive doctrine by which the Reformation was rendered possible; for the Reformation on its theological and religious side was just an Augustinian revival. . . . For what was the Reformation inwardly considered, but the triumph of Augustine's doctrine of grace over Augustine's doctrine of the Church?"

3. Will Durant, *The Age of Faith* (New York: Simon and Schuster, 1950), 75.

4. Augustine, *The Literal Meaning of Genesis,* vol. 1 (New York: Paulist Press, 1982), 41.

5. Augustine, *Sermons on the Old Testament (20–50),* The Works of Saint Augustine (New York: New City Press, 1990), 2:240.

6. Augustine, *The Confessions of St. Augustine* (Edinburgh: T&T Clark, 1876), 1.

7. This is a modernized version of *Nicene and Post-Nicene Fathers of the Christian Church* (NPNF), ed. Philip Schaff (New York: The Christian Literature Company, 1892). NPNF[1], 12:504.

8. Augustine, *The Confessions of St. Augustine,* 3.5.9.

9. Augustine, *Augustine: Later Works* (Philadelphia: The Westminster Press, 1955), 317.

10. Augustine, *City of God,* 21.8.2.

11. Augustine, *The Works of Aurelius Augustine,* vol. 9 (Edinburgh: T&T Clark, 1883), 24.

12. Augustine, *Confessions of Saint Augustine* (New York: J. M. Dent & Sons, 1920), 20.

13. For a helpful overview of why Augustine was attracted to celibacy, see Veronica Arntz, "Pursuing Asceticism: St. Augustine & St. Anthony of Egypt," Catholic Exchange, January 17, 2018, https://catholicexchange.com/pursuing -asceticism-st-augustine-st-anthony-egypt.

14. According to David G. Hunter, ed., *Marriage and Sexuality in Early Christianity* (Minneapolis: Fortress Press, 2018), 32, Augustine made a distinction between two types of concupiscence. There was a proper type of sexual desire in marriage, and then there is a fleshly sinful sexual desire. Regardless, he did not disparage marriage. He believed it was honorable and permissible. For Augustine, marriage was a good thing. A position that radically differed from other theologians of his day (like Jerome and Ambrose) who viewed marriage as a negative aspect of the fall.

15. *Against Faustus,* book 15, 7, in NPNF[1] 4:216.

16. *Christian History* 6, no. 3: 26–28.

17. Augustine, *Confessions,* 11.3.

18. *NPNF¹* 5:62. In this brief section, Augustine is discussing why children should be baptized. He says that through baptism, children are "freed from the serpent's poisonous bite."

19. *NPNF¹* 5:404.

20. *NPNF¹* 3:374–75.

21. *Christian History* 4, no. 3: 29.

22. Augustine, *The Correction of the Donatists*, 22–24; also see *NPNF¹* 4:642.

23. *NPNF¹* I, 388.

24. *NPNF¹* I, 470.

25. *On Forgiveness of Sins and Baptism*, 1:34. in *NPNF¹* 5:28. Note: the primitive apostolic tradition being spoken of was referring to the sacraments as "salvation" and "life." Augustine went on to discuss the testimony of Scripture. Whatever Augustine meant by "impossible," Schaff argues Augustine did not adhere to transubstantiation, but he rather held to some sort of "real spiritual participation." *NPNF¹* 1:388–99.

26. *The Anti-Nicene Fathers (ANF)*, ed. Rev. Alexander Roberts and James Donaldson (New York: Charles Scribner's Son, 1905), 3:246.

27. See chapter 10 of my book with George Barna, *Pagan Christianity*, for the history of Christian education.

28. *NPNF¹* 5:475. For Augustine, some people are granted perseverance to the end (or elected to persevere to the end) while others are not.

Augustine wrote *De correptione et gratia*, where he explicitly rejects this conclusion and affirms the necessity of correction and rebuke for fallen believers. The first section of this treatise treats the efficacy of grace and the importance of discipline and admonition in the Christian life. The remaining portion of the work concerns the grace of perseverance and the consequent role of moral living of the believer. In Augustine's own opinion, *De correptione et gratia* is his fullest and best expression of the gratuitous nature of God's persevering one to the end. He argues here that a believer who loses his faith bears the sole blame for such a loss, but one who retains faith demonstrates the gift of persevering grace. He further argues that no one of the elect perishes—those who in life fall away are, and forever have been, part of the reprobate. On the other hand, if one of the elect were to fall away, God would necessarily insure that that person will eventually repent and return to the church. Augustine does not try to delve into the mysteries of why God grants perseverance to some and not to others, but rests upon Paul's words, "Oh the depth of the riches of the wisdom and knowledge of God!" (Romans 11:33). The core teaching of this treatise, however, that one's perseverance to the end is solely a work of grace by God, is vividly expressed throughout. It was to defend this understanding of the completely gratuitous nature of persevering grace that led Augustine to write his final work on perseverance, *De dono perseverantiae*. Henry Knapp, "Augustine and Owen on Preservation," *Westminster Theological Journal* 62 (2000): 65–88.

29. *Enchiridion of Faith, Hope, and Love*, chapter 107 in *NPNF¹* vol. 3.

30. St. Augustine, *Sermons on the Liturgical Seasons*, The Fathers of the Church, vol. 38 (Washington, DC: The Catholic University of America, 1959), 10.

31. Luigi Gambero, *Mary and the Fathers of the Church: The Blessed Virgin Mary in Patristic Thought* (San Francisco: Ignatius Press, 1999), 224.

32. *Of Holy Virginity*, sec. 4; *NPNF¹* 3:418.

33. Joseph Berington and John Kirk, *The Faith of Catholics*, vol. 1 (New York: Fr. Pustet & Co., 1909), 431.

34. William A. Jurgens, ed. and trans., *The Faith of the Early Fathers* (Collegeville, MN: Liturgical Press, 1970 and 1979), 3:29.

35. Augustine, *City of God*, 21, 24, 2; *NPNF¹* 2:470. In a footnote at this point in *NPNF¹* 2 from Schaff: "This contains the germ of the doctrine of purgatory, which was afterwards more fully developed by Pope Gregory I, and adopted by the Roman church, but rejected by the Reformers as unfounded in Scripture, through Matt. Xii, 32, and I Cor. Iii. 15, are quoted in support of it."

36. See Douglas Moo's commentary on Romans in the New International Commentary on the New Testament (NICNT) for an excellent discussion on Romans 5:12 via Augustine et al. In Moo's last point, he speaks of "corporate solidarity," how the actions of certain individuals could have a "representative character" (Douglas Moo, *The Letter to the Romans*, NICNT [Grand Rapids: Eerdmans, 2018], 327). So while Moo discusses the translation difficulties, he doesn't appear to deny Augustine's overall position.

37. Charles Finney, *Lectures on Systematic Theology* (New York: George H. Doran Company, 1878), 252.

38. Whitney Oates, *Basic Writings of Saint Augustine*, vol. 2, *City of God* (New York: Random House Publishers, 1948), 564–66. His words were, "If, therefore, the salamander lives in fire, as naturalists have recorded, and if certain famous mountains of Sicily have been continually on fire from the remotest antiquity until now, and yet remain entire, these are sufficiently convincing examples that everything which burns is not consumed. As the soul too, is a proof that not everything which can suffer pain can also die, why then do they yet demand that we produce real examples to prove that it is not incredible that the bodies of men condemned to everlasting punishment may retain their soul in the fire, may burn without being consumed, and may suffer without perishing?" (*NPNF¹* 2:454).

39. Augustine, *The Retractions* (Washington, DC: The Catholic University Press of America, 1968), 169.

Chapter 11 The Shocking Beliefs of John Wesley

1. *Christian History* 11, no. 1: 4.

2. Wesley's wife, Mary Vazeille (known as Molly), vehemently opposed her husband. For details, see Stephen Tomkins, *John Wesley: A Biography* (Grand Rapids: Eerdmans, 2003), 155–74; Nathan Busenitz, *John Wesley's Failed Marriage* (published on The Cripple Gate website); Lillian Harvey, *John Wesley and His Wife* (Richmond, KY: Harvey Christian Publishers, n.d.).

3. *C. H. Spurgeon's Autobiography*, vol. 1 (London: Passmore and Alabaster, 1899), 176.

4. J. C. Ryle, *Christian Leaders of the Last Century* (London: T. Nelson and Sons, 1869), 105.

5. Rev. L. Tyerman, *The Life and Times of John Wesley*, vol. 2 (London: Hodder and Stoughton, 1872), 363.

6. *The Works of the Rev. John Wesley*, vol. 5 (New York: Carlton & Phillips, 1853), 235. See also *Christian History* 2, no. 1: 4.

7. *The Miscellaneous Works of Adam Clarke* (Glasgow: R. Griffin and Co., 1836), 287–88; H. Newton Malony Jr., *The Amazing John Wesley: An Unusual Look at an Uncommon Life* (Downers Grove, IL: InterVarsity, 2010), 12.

8. In John Wesley's "Letter to a Roman Catholic," Dublin, July 18, 1749, in John Wesley, *Works of the Rev. John Wesley*, vol. 10 (London: John Mason, City-Road, 1860), 81.

9. Malony Jr., *Amazing John Wesley*, 159.

10. John Wesley, *Primitive Physick* (Leeds: Web & Millington, 1846), 12.

11. Wesley, *Primitive Physick*, 9.

12. Malony Jr., *Amazing John Wesley*, 72–73. For his many cures, see Wesley, *Primitive Physick*.

13. Wesley, *Primitive Physick*, 9.

14. Wesley, *Works of John Wesley*, 3:247; "Advice to the People Called Methodists with Regard to Dress," *The Works of the Reverend John Wesley*, vol. 6 (New York: Waugh and T. Mason, 1835), 546–47.

15. J. Parnell McCarter, "On Jewelry and Attire: 'Put Off Thy Ornaments from Thee,'" *Puritan News Weekly*, April 6, 2004.

16. J. B. Galloway, *A Study of Holiness from the Early Church Fathers* (Eugene, OR: Wipf & Stock, 2014), 33.

17. John Wesley, *The Works of John Wesley*, vol. 11 (Grand Rapids: Zondervan, 1872), 485–86.

Chapter 12 The Shocking Beliefs of Charles Spurgeon

1. *Christian History* 10, no. 1: 2.

2. *Spurgeon's Fast Day Services, Held in the Sydenham Crystal Palace on October 7, 1857* (Melbourne: Smith Bookseller and Stationer, 1858). It is estimated that he preached to over ten million people throughout his life. This estimate appears to be from the calculations of Arthur Tappan Pierson. According to this author,

> I was making a computation, and I found that he must have preached the gospel, during the time of his public ministry, to no less than ten millions of people; that during his pastorate he must have received into communion between ten and twelve thousand converts; that his sermons must have reached a total of between twenty and forty millions of readers during the last thirty years; and that, probably, to-day there are over fifty millions of people that are reading the account of his life, and his labours, and his decease and burial. (*From the Pulpit to the Palm Branch* [New York: A. C. Armstrong and Son, 1892], 229)

See also *Christian History* 10, no. 1: 2–3.

3. Russell Herman Cornwell, *Life of Charles Haddon Spurgeon, The World's Greatest Preacher* (New York: Edgewood Publishing, 1892), 235.

4. Christian George, *The Lost Sermons of C. H. Spurgeon, Volume 1: His Earliest Outlines and Sermons Between 1851 and 1854* (Nashville: B&H Academic, 2017), xvii–xx; Matt Carter and Aaron Ivey, *Steal Away Home: Charles Spurgeon*

and Thomas Jefferson: Unlikely Friends on the Passage to Freedom (Nashville: B&H Publishing, 2017).

5. Charles H. Spurgeon, *The Sword and the Trowel*, vol. 4 (London: Passmore and Alibaster, 1874), 111–13, 116. Alternate text: C. H. *Spurgeon's Autobiography*, vol. 1 (London: Passmore and Alabaster, 1899), 355–56.

6. G. Holden Pike, *The Life and Work of Charles Haddon Spurgeon*, vol. 5 (London: Cassel, 1923), 138–40. See also W. M. Hutchings, *Smoking to the Glory of God: A Letter to the Rev. C. H. Spurgeon in Reply to His Apology for Smoking, with Special Reference to the Principle on Which That Apology Is Based*, 2nd ed. (London: W. M. Hutchings, 1874), 5-7-14; Charles Ray, *The Life of Charles Haddon Spurgeon* (London: Passmore and Alabaster, 1903), 490–91.

7. Quoted in Justin D. Fulton, *Charles H. Spurgeon, Our Ally* (Chicago: H. J. Smith & Co., 1892), 345.

8. *The Autobiography of Charles H. Spurgeon*, vol. 3 (London: Passmore and Alabaster, 1899), 138. For Spurgeon on debt, see also Charles Spurgeon, *John Ploughman's Talk* (Philadelphia: Henry Altemus, 1896), 96–110.

9. Spurgeon, *John Ploughman's Talk*, 183, 210–11. In this quote, Spurgeon is speaking via his character "John Ploughman."

10. Spurgeon, *John Ploughman's Talk*, 16–17. In this quote, Spurgeon is speaking via his character "John Ploughman."

11. Reginald H. Barnes, *Charles Haddon Spurgeon: The People's Preacher* (Kilmarnock, Scotland: John Ritchie, Ltd., Publishers of Christian Literature, 1892), 235–36.

12. W. Y. Fullerton, *C. H. Spurgeon: A Biography* (London: Williams and Norgate, 1920), 260.

13. Christian George, "How Would Spurgeon Vote?" Nov. 7, 2016, published in the Spurgeon Center; *Christian History* 10, no. 1: 13.

14. *C. H. Spurgeon's Autobiography*, vol. 4 (London: Passmore and Alabaster, 1900), 127.

15. Christian George, "How Would Spurgeon Vote?" Nov. 7, 2016, published in the Spurgeon Center.

16. Timothy Weber, "The Baptist Tradition," in *Curing and Caring: Health and Medicine In the Western Faith Traditions*, ed. Ronald L. Numbers and Darryl W. Amundsen (Baltimore: John Hopkins University Press, 1986), 294; Conwell, *Life of Charles Haddon Spurgeon*, 173–79.

17. Conwell, *Life of Charles Haddon Spurgeon*, 184–85. See also Conwell, chapter 3, on Spurgeon's experience with miracles.

18. *C. H. Spurgeon's Autobiography*, vol. 1 (London: Passmore and Alabaster, 1899), 362. See Spurgeon's two sermons, "The Minister's Fainting Fits," *Charles Spurgeon, Lectures to My Students, First Series* (New York: Robert Carter & Brothers, 1890), 249–67; and "The Desire of the Soul in Spiritual Darkness," *C. H. Spurgeon, The New Park Street Pulpit*, vol. 1 (Grand Rapids: Zondervan, 1963), 237–44. Also see *Christian History* 10, no. 1: 22–25.

19. Conwell, *Life of Charles Haddon Spurgeon*, 85.

20. *C. H. Spurgeon's Autobiography*, vol. 1 (London: Passmore and Alabaster, 1899), 242.

21. *C. H. Spurgeon's Autobiography*, vol. 3 (London: Passmore and Alabaster, 1899), 89; and W. Y. Fullerton, *C. H. Spurgeon: A Biography* (London: Williams and Norgate, 1920), 250. Note that Spurgeon was a Reformed Baptist; however, he got into heated disputes with at least one hyper-Calvinist. See Iain Murray, *The Forgotten Spurgeon* (Edinburgh: Banner of Trust, 2010); and Iain Murray, *Spurgeon v. Hyper-Calvinism* (Edinburgh: Banner of Truth Trust, 2010).

22. This quote appears in a story recounted by Spurgeon's associate, Godfrey Holden Pike. See Pike, *Charles Haddon Spurgeon, Preacher, Author, Philanthropist* (New York: Funk & Wagnalls, 1892), 335–36.

Chapter 13 The Shocking Beliefs of D. L. Moody

1. *Christian History* 9, no. 1.

2. William R. Moody, *The Life of D. L. Moody* (New York: Fleming H. Revell Company, 1900), 43.

3. Moody, *Life of D. L. Moody*, 568.

4. G. Campbell Morgan, "Christ and Nathanael," *The Advance* 54 (Dec. 26, 1907): 789.

5. Paul Dwight Moody and Percy L. Fitt, *The Shorter Life of D. L. Moody*, vol. 1: *His Life* (Chicago: The Bible Institute Colportage Association, 1900), 95.

6. *The New Sermons of Dwight Lyman Moody* (New York: Henry S. Goodspeed, 1880), 589.

7. James F. Findlay, *Dwight L. Moody, American Evangelist 1837–1899* (Eugene, OR: Wipf & Stock, 1969), 40.

8. Warren W. Wiersbe, *50 People Every Christian Should Know* (Grand Rapids: Baker Books, 2014), 2009, 177–78.

9. Alton Gansky, *60 People Who Shaped the Church* (Grand Rapids: Baker Books, 2014), 275–76. For further insight into Moody's life, see *Christian History* 9, no. 1; Gansky, *60 People*, chap. 53; Wiersbe, *50 People*, chap. 24; Moody, *The Life of D. L. Moody*.

10. Dwight L. Moody, *The New Sermons of Dwight Lyman Moody* (New York: Nelson & Phillips, 1877), 258.

11. D. L. Moody, *Great Joy* (New York: EB Treat, 1877), 183.

12. *Christian History* 9, no. 1: 19.

13. Dwight L. Moody, "When My Lord Jesus Comes," *The Herald of Gospel Liberty* 8, no. 28 (July 13, 1911): 878 (9).

14. "Drummond's Greatest Thing in the World," *Christianity Today*, April 28, 2010; D. W. Bebbington, "Henry Drummond, Evangelicalism and Science," Internet Archive, 145–46.

Some of Drummond's opinions caused other evangelicals to refuse to appear on stage with him during Moody's 1893 Northfield Conference.

15. *Christian History* 9, no. 1: 25; Rosemary Skinner Kelley and Rosemary Radford Reuther, eds., *Encyclopedia of Women and Religion in North America* (Indianapolis: Indiana University Press, 2006), 441.

16. Richard Turnbull, *A Passionate Faith: What Makes an Evangelical* (Oxford, UK: Monarch Books, 2012), 146.

17. Dwight L. Moody, *The Gospel Awakening* (Chicago: Fleming H. Revell, 1883), 370.

18. D. L. Moody, *One Thousand and One Thoughts from My Library* (Chicago: Fleming H. Revell, 1898), 15, 113.

19. Martyn McGeown, "The Life and Theology of D. L. Moody" on the Covenant Protestant Reformed website.

20. D. L. Moody, *Weighed and Wanting* (Chicago: The Bible Institute Colportage Association, 1898), 15.

21. D. L. Moody, "How Shall We Spend the Sabbath?" *Golden Counsels* (Boston: United Society of Christian Endeavor, 1899); D. L. Moody, *The Ten Commandments: Reasonable Rules for Life* (Kensington, PA: Whitaker House, 2016).

22. D. L. Moody, *Heaven: Where It Is, Its Inhabitants, And How to Get There* (New York: Fleming H. Revell, 1884), 35.

Chapter 14 Seven Shocking Statements by Billy Graham

1. Franklin Graham, "My Father Has Gone Home," and Cathy Lynn Grossman, "Evangelist Blazed Numerous Spiritual Trails," *USA Today*, Feb. 22, 2018.

2. Billy Graham, interview by Robert Schuller, *Hour of Power*, May 31, 1997. This interview can also be construed as Graham saying that there are people involved in false religions that are called by God who will eventually be called out of those religions and brought into the church later after they hear and respond to the gospel.

3. Billy Graham, "I Can't Play God Anymore," interview with James M. Beam, *McCall's*, January 1978, 156, 158. It should be noted that according to one source, Graham issued this clarification about the above interview:

> On the whole, I am pleased with the accuracy of the interview. However, a few of the statements unfortunately convey meanings which I never intended to suggest in the original, unedited interview. This may be due to my own failure to make myself as plain as I should have. Whoever sees the footsteps of the Creator in nature can ask the God he does not fully know for help, and I believe God—in ways we may not fully understand—will give that person further light and bring him to a knowledge of the truth that is in Jesus Christ so he will be saved. More significantly, however, Graham did not repudiate his views about Roman Catholicism. These views explain why he uses Roman Catholics as counselors in his evangelistic campaigns, why he urged Catholics to reconfirm their confirmation at his 1979 rally in Milwaukee, why the Vatican would not oppose a Graham campaign in Rome, why he does not tell Catholic "converts" that they should leave their parish churches, and why there is now adequate evidence to question Billy Graham's belief of the truth. Paul curses anyone who perverts or preaches any other Gospel than that which Paul preached, and Christians ought to take such curses seriously. (Published on The Trinity Foundation website at the end of an article called "Dispensationalism" by Gordon H. Clark)

4. Bruce Buursma, "Concerns of the Evangelist," *Christianity Today*, April 5, 1985; "What I Would Have Done Differently," *Christianity Today*, Billy Graham's regrets, in his own words, compiled by Collin Hansen, April 2018, p. 95.

5. Billy Graham, interview by Sarah Pulliam Bailey, *Christianity Today*, January 21, 2011.

6. Billy Graham, interview by Greta Van Susteren, November 7, 2011.

7. Billy Graham, *World Aflame* (United Kingdom: World's Work, 1965), 86.

8. Billy Graham, "Billy Graham Speaks: The Evangelical World Prospect," an exclusive interview in *Christianity Today* 3, no. 1 (Oct. 13, 1958): 5.

Chapter 16 You Just Might Be a Pharisee If . . .

1. E. Stanley Jones, *The Way* (Nashville: Abingdon Press, 2015), Week 19, Wednesday.

Chapter 17 Twenty Reasons Why the Christian Right and the Christian Left Won't Adopt Me

1. Rick Warren, interview, *This Week with George Stephanopoulos*, ABC News, April 8, 2012.

Chapter 23 The Essentials of Our Faith

1. radicalresurgence.com/essentials.

2. C. S. Lewis, *Mere Christianity* (London: William Collins, 1952), viii.

3. Frank Viola, *Reimagining Church* (Colorado Springs: David C. Cook, 2008), 237–38.

Chapter 24 Who Are the Real Heretics?

1. Ben Witherington, *Grace in Galatia: A Commentary on St. Paul's Letter to the Galatians* (Grand Rapids: Eerdmans, 1998), 401.

Chapter 25 They Are Our Teachers

1. Lewis, *Collected Letters*, 119.

2. Jonathan Edwards, *Charity and Its Fruits* (New York: Robert Carter & Brothers, 1852), 243–44.

3. Martin Luther, *Luther's Large Catechism*, trans. John N. Lenker, vol. 2, Christian Educational Series (Minneapolis: Luther Press, 1908), 123–24.

4. John Calvin, *Institutes of the Christian Religion* (Philadelphia: The Westminster Press, 1960), 4.17.32.

5. Augustine, *The Literal Meaning of Genesis*, vol. 1 (New York: Paulist Press, 1982), 41.

6. John Wesley, *The Works of John Wesley, Volume 1: Sermons 1–53* (Harrington, DE: Delmarva Publications, 2014).

7. Charles Spurgeon, "Satanic Hindrances," The Spurgeon Center, October 29, 1865, Metropolitan Tabernacle Pulpit, https://www.spurgeon.org/resource-library/sermons/satanic-hindrances#flipbook/.

8. D. L. Moody, *The D. L. Moody Collection* (Karpathos Collections, 2015).

9. Billy Graham, "True Unity," Daily Devotion, Billy Graham Evangelistic Association, July 2, https://billygraham.org/devotion/true-unity/.

Frank Viola has helped thousands of people around the world to deepen their relationship with Jesus Christ and enter into a more vibrant and authentic experience of church. He has written many books on these themes, including his signature work, *Insurgence: Reclaiming the Gospel of the Kingdom*. His blog, frankviola.org, is ranked in the top ten of all Christian blogs on the web today.

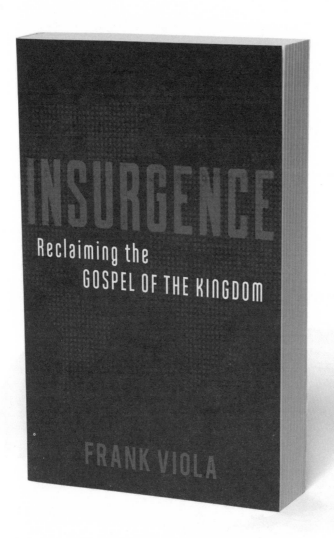

"In this insightful and transformative book, Frank Viola reveals with crystal clarity just how far removed our truncated gospel is from the kingdom of God that Jesus embodied and that He calls and empowers His followers to embody."

—GREG BOYD,
pastor and author